Sentencing

This book examines the process and purpose of sentencing in the criminal justice system, beyond the confines of its legalistic aspects.

Sentencing is the process that concludes any criminal trial that ends with the defendant being convicted, and any hearing in which a defendant pleads guilty. Those convicted of crime have been subject to sentencing as the method of imposing a punishment for their offences since the earliest existence of anything we would recognise as a criminal justice system. Yet the rationale behind sentencing, and the process by which it happens, has long been viewed through a traditional lens. In contrast, this book considers not just the process by which a Judge arrives at a numerical sentence of months in custody or the amount of a fine, but the wider meanings and effects of sentencing, as seen through the lens of various ideas of social justice.

The book will appeal to students, academics, and legal practitioners who wish to consider a different perspective on the well-known and well-researched, but often shifting, area of sentencing.

Elaine A. O. Freer is a College Teaching Officer and Fellow in Law at Robinson College, Cambridge, UK, and a practising barrister at 5 Paper Buildings (Chambers of Miranda Moore QC and Julian Christopher QC).

Part of the
NEW TRAJECTORIES IN LAW
series

series editors
Adam Gearey, Birkbeck College, University of London
Colin Perrin, Commissioning Editor, Routledge

for information about the series and details of previous and forthcoming
titles, see
https://www.routledge.com/New-Trajectories-in-Law/book-series/NTL

A GlassHouse Book

Sentencing

New Trajectories in Law

Elaine A. O. Freer

Routledge
Taylor & Francis Group
a GlassHouse Book

First published 2021
by Routledge
2 Park Square, Milton Park, Abingdon, Oxon OX14 4RN

and by Routledge
605 Third Avenue, New York, NY 10158

A GlassHouse Book

Routledge is an imprint of the Taylor & Francis Group, an informa business

British Library Cataloguing-in-Publication Data
A catalogue record for this book is available from the British Library

Library of Congress Cataloging-in-Publication Data
A catalog record has been requested for this book

ISBN: 978-0-367-86261-9 (hbk)
ISBN: 978-1-032-06302-7 (pbk)
ISBN: 978-1-003-20162-5 (ebk)

Typeset in Times New Roman
by Deanta Global Publishing Services, Chennai, India

Most of this book was written during the coronavirus pandemic. It is therefore dedicated to my 'lockdown family', both two- and four-legged:

Jim, Ben, Claudia, Jacqui, Jo, Kim, Mark, Nikki, and Sarah

and

Beau, Buddy, Clyde, Duke, Iris, Sawyer, Scooby, and Trug

It is also dedicated to the memory of
His Honour Judge Stuart Bridge
(1958–2020)

The most patient and good-humoured supervisor of Land Law and a thoroughly kind, fair, and decent Judge.

Contents

Foreword

I am delighted to write a foreword to this book. Elaine has taken the opportunity to share her thoughts on sentencing law and theory, by juxtaposing examples from her practice as a barrister in the criminal courts. In doing this, she demonstrates, very clearly, how theory, law, and practice can lead us in quite different directions, and down surprisingly different paths. This book is full of vignettes from real life, which Elaine uses to develop her own critique of traditional theories of punishment. The 'stories' are endlessly diverting – from the sad case of the homeless man who can't have any treatment requirements added to his community order simply because he is homeless (p. 64) to the realistic magistrates who decided not to send a man back to prison, for the good reason that it didn't work last time (p. 65). They are also deeply depressing – the sentencing options are so limited, and the resort to imprisonment so common.

Sentencers know that imprisonment is rarely an effective outcome. This book gives revealing insights into the 'stories', not only of the sentenced, but also of those who do the sentencing. We get hints at attempts at real conversations, as judges and magistrates try to communicate their fears and anxieties, and indeed their frustrations (with offenders and with the system which has let them down). There are also hopes: for example, repeated hope that this defendant will not come back to court (and will not 'let the judge down' as one judge puts it, when he defers sentencing a defendant telling him that he, the judge, is taking a risk with his own reputation by doing this).

Elaine tells us that OT's case was part of the inspiration for this book. OT's 'story' includes his victim's wife who told him at the end of the hearing that, had her husband known everything said in mitigation, he would have strenuously opposed the police charging OT. Well done Mrs Victim! Her voice deserves to be heard: victims are often not as 'punitive' as politicians think. She recognised that the criminal court was not the right place for OT. Criminal courts are awkward and uncomfortable places where those who break the law, their victims, the public (very rarely in evidence), and judges/magistrates come together – and then the judge or magistrates make a hugely important decision which all too often does little to put right what went wrong, in any sense.

Sentencing involves a complex web of decision-making. These summaries of sentencing remarks tell a story of human interactions: judges and magistrates attempting to sentence people in ways which both fit within the legal 'framework' but which also make some sort of sense in the reality of that particular court room encounter, at that particular moment in time. Sentencing Guidelines may help police and prosecutors make better charging decisions, and may help judges and magistrates edge their way towards consistent sentencing outcomes. But it is the sentencer alone who bears the heavy burden of reaching what appears to be the appropriate and individualised 'response' to the individual in front of them.

The aims of sentencing, well explained in this book, are often contradictory. Sentencers receive these complex messages. Public protection, rehabilitation, punishment, reparation, and deterrence – these words bubble around. This book, with its focus on the reality of the challenges which are faced by both sentencers and those they sentence, is a very welcome addition to the literature.

Nicola Padfield
Professor of Penal & Criminal Justice, University of Cambridge
Life & Honorary Fellow, Fitzwilliam College, Cambridge

Preface

My interest in sentencing is formed from two different angles: academic and practitioner. As an academic, I want to examine and critique the legislation, guidelines, and theory that are applied when dealing with someone who has been convicted of a criminal offence. Having undertaken an MPhil in Criminology, and since 2012 having taught undergraduates taking the Criminology, Sentencing and the Penal System Course as part of the Law Tripos at Cambridge, I have had many opportunities to discuss and reflect on sentencing law and practice. As a practitioner, I use the legislation and guidelines when I am advising my clients, whether that is a lay client, or a professional client – a defence solicitor or reviewing lawyer from a prosecuting agency. Often theory and practice lead to quite different results, and it is in these collisions between theory and practice that I am especially interested.

The research base of this book is my own cases. They are not a representative sample of cases passing through criminal courts, but are included to provide colour and life to illustrate the principles and requirements of modern-day sentencing. Often it is less serious cases, where there are real questions about what sort of sentence should be passed – whether it should be a custodial sentence or not, and if so, whether it can be suspended – that pose a greater challenge to a sentencer in pinpointing a just and proportionate sentence than those cases which are so serious that the only possible sentence is lengthy custody.

I began practising as a barrister, as a 'second six' pupil, in April 2016, and continue to practise from the same chambers. My practice is almost entirely criminal – mixed defence and prosecution. All the sentencing remarks used in this book are from cases where I was the advocate at the sentence hearing. Where details of a case are included, those details were in either the prosecution's opening, or in the defence's mitigation, and all of the sentencing remarks were made in open court, where any member of the public or the press could have been present. Therefore, although I was making a contemporaneous (and, as far as possible, verbatim) note because I was the advocate and needed to provide it to those instructing me, any member of the public or press could have published any of the details used in this book. Therefore, I have not revealed anything not already in the public domain. However, I have nonetheless anonymised the cases, referring to them by initials of the defendant, date, and court where the hearing took place. The sentencing comments as seen in this book are faithful reproductions from my contemporaneous notes; however, they are not a transcript and occasionally words in square brackets have been added in for sense. Almost all sentencing remarks featured in this book were delivered *ex tempore*, sometimes in the context of a busy list where the sentencing Judge or bench of magistrates had tens of cases in their list for the day. In that context there is much to admire in the detail and clarity seen in many of the remarks, which have a hugely varied audience: lawyers, defendants, victims, press, and public.

Appellate court judgments in sentencing appeals have been available in reported cases for many years. More recently a greater volume has been available with neutral citations via free websites such as bailii.org. Meanwhile, everyday sentencing hearings that form such a big part of the criminal justice system remain largely unreported, unless they are nationally high-profile, or hold a certain interest within a local area, usually due to particularly serious or striking facts, or the involvement of someone well-known.

My aim in this book, however, is to examine what can be understood by the five aims and objectives that must be considered by the Judge in every sentencing process of an adult offender (someone over the age of 18)[1] as required by section 57(2)(a)–(e) of the Sentencing Act 2020:[2] punishment, deterrence, rehabilitation, protection, and reparation. I examine them as concepts in their own right, how they interact with one another, and how we see them brought to life in various legislative provisions that are relevant to sentencing, such as the aggravating effect of previous convictions, or the mandatory minimum sentences for those who repeatedly commit certain types of offences. I also try to capture something of how 'everyday' sentencing exercises, in routine cases across the country, exhibit the aims and

---

1 This book does not consider the aims of the youth justice system and those applicable to young offenders due to constraints of space.
2 This was formerly s.142 of the Criminal Justice Act 2003 – this book will be published after 1st December 2020, when the Sentencing Act 2020 comes into force, and thus section numbers given are from the 2020 Act. The previous section number and Act will be given in a footnote the first time the provision is encountered.

objectives of sentencing that the legislature intended. In doing so it gives an insight into how the legislation is brought into play – how the theory and practice coincide or collide. Writing this book illustrated how expressive some Judge's sentencing remarks are, and the amount of thought that is put into sentencing exercises which, although routine and mundane to the Judge, recognise the humanity behind the facts – the offender, the victim, their respective families, and the wider communities involved.

Acknowledgements

Since 2012 I have been discussing sentencing with undergraduate students to whom I have taught Criminology, Sentencing and the Penal System from Selwyn, St John's, Jesus, Girton, Sidney Sussex, and Robinson Colleges, and Hughes Hall, at the University of Cambridge. Over the years these discussions have provided huge inspiration and provoked me to think about sentencing's aims from different perspectives. I owe all of those students my thanks for the role they played in shaping my thoughts through our lively supervisions.

Tales from my chambers' colleagues of particularly moving sentencing remarks that they had heard turned my thoughts to using first instance courts' sentencing remarks as the basis for such an exploration.

In showcasing 'everyday' sentencing, this book also highlights the thoughtfulness and gravity with which most lay magistrates and Judges approach sentencing exercises. Without the efforts put into their daily sentencing decisions, reflected in the remarks made when passing sentence, there could have been no book. Against huge challenges in the criminal justice system, that these efforts continue is worthy of note and acknowledgement.

On a personal level I am grateful to Robert O'Sullivan QC for his assiduous proofreading, and to him, my parents, and colleagues at both Robinson College and 5 Paper Buildings for their support whilst I have been working on this book.

Introduction

Sentencing disposals in England and Wales

This book is not a systematic analysis of sentencing comments made in certain courts or in certain types of cases. What it is seeking to do, in keeping with the spirit of the New Trajectories in Law series, is to examine sentencing from an angle that is often ignored. That is, to look at everyday sentencing exercises in first instance courts across England. This book aims to explore sentencing in an engaging way by bringing in legislation, literature, and theory from a variety of sources, gathered through the prism of the single section of legislation that sets out the aims and objectives to which every Judge sentencing for a criminal offence must have regard: s.57(2)(a)–(e) of the Sentencing Act 2020. It looks at Judges' reasons, and discusses what those reasons tell us about how the considerations required by s.57(2) affect the sentences that Judges give.

It in no way claims to be an exhaustive treatise of all possible theoretical underpinnings to sentencing. Its purpose is instead to look at (though not venture a conclusive answer to) the 'bigger questions' about sentencing. It does this by combining sentencing comments made by Judges in real cases with a variety of legislation, discussion of guidelines, and theories. Its aim is to provoke thought as much as to answer questions.

Before looking at how first instance sentencing exercises exhibit and interpret the aims and objectives of the legislature, it is important to know a little of how sentencing works in theory. This introduction, therefore, sets out the groundwork through applicable legislation and Sentencing Guidelines. It does not attempt to cover all sentencing law, that being a vast corpus of disparate provisions. It also introduces the main forms of sentence that a defendant being sentenced in England may receive. With these matters of law and procedure covered at the outset, the rest of the book provides an examination of sentencing exercises without interruption by explanations of technical terms.

DOI: 10.4324/9781003201625-101

The sentencing process[1]

Sentencing concludes any criminal case in which the defendant has pleaded guilty, or been found guilty. A finding of guilt can be made by two or three lay magistrates or a District Judge in the Magistrates' Court, or a jury in the Crown Court. Very occasionally, a Judge will sit without a jury in the Crown Court, and reach a verdict on their own.[2] Many defendants,[3] however, admit their guilt without a trial – they 'plead guilty'. Sometimes this is done 'on the full facts' – that is, they admit the misconduct that the prosecution alleges. Other times it is done 'on a basis' – the defendant admits that they committed the crime alleged, but they do not accept important parts of the prosecution's case. Where this happens, it is for the Judge to decide whether the difference between what the Crown[4] alleges, and what the defendant accepts, is sufficiently significant that it would affect sentence. If it does not, then the difference does not need to be resolved. If it does, then there will be a 'Newton hearing' – a mini trial of the specific issue about which there is disagreement, at which the Judge decides the factual basis for sentence.[5]

The sentence imposed in the Magistrates' Court is decided by either lay magistrates advised by a legally trained clerk, or a District Judge. There are specific Sentencing Guidelines that apply in the Magistrates' Court (for more on Sentencing Guidelines, see below). The maximum sentence that can be imposed in the Magistrates' Court by any tribunal is one of six months' imprisonment (whether immediate or suspended) for a single offence,[6] or

---

1 This book concerns the sentencing system in England and Wales, and wherever England is referred to, this should be read to include Wales. Scotland and Northern Ireland have separate systems with significant differences.

2 There are a very limited set of circumstances in which a person may be found guilty in the Crown Court by a Judge only – these are usually where there has been jury tampering – see s.44 Criminal Justice Act 2003, and, as an example, the case of *J* [2010] EWCA Crim 1755. There is a further power in s.43 of the CJA 2003 for trial by Judge alone in cases of serious fraud, but this has never been brought into force.

3 The rate of guilty pleas in the last quarter before coronavirus, which has a distorting effect on the figures, was around 70% in the Crown Court: Ministry of Justice (2020) Criminal court statistics quarterly, England and Wales, January to March 2020, London: Ministry of Justice, at p. 9. Available at https://assets.publishing.service.gov.uk/government/uploads/system/uploads/attachment_data/file/895063/ccsq_bulletin_jan_mar_2020.pdf [accessed 25th November 2020].

4 In this text 'Crown' is synonymous with 'prosecution'.

5 Named after the case of *Newton* [1983] CrimLR 198.

6 S.78(1) of the Powers of the Criminal Courts (Sentencing) Act 2000 ('PCC(S)A 00'). Section 154 of the Criminal Justice Act 2003 ('CJA 03') raises the maximum for a single offence to 12 months, but it has never been brought into force.

a maximum of 12 months for multiple 'triable either way'[7] offences.[8] If the Magistrates' Court does not have sufficient sentencing powers for the offence's seriousness, then the offence will be 'committed for sentence' – it goes to the Crown Court, where the Judge can sentence up to the maximum permitted by statute for the offence.

A defendant being sentenced in the Crown Court will be sentenced by a Judge alone – the jury play no part in sentencing. For offences often tried in the Crown Court, there are separate, offence-specific guidelines, again published by the Sentencing Council. The most severe form of punishment which a Judge sitting in the Crown Court can impose is imprisonment – capital punishment in England and Wales having been abolished in 1969.[9]

Types of sentence

Through the Sentencing Act 2020 ('SA 20'), which came into force on 1st December 2020, all aspects of sentencing law are now found in one consolidating statute. The content of the sentencing legislation now appearing in the SA 20 has not changed.

There are six main types of sentence available in English law, the principal features of which are set out here, from the least to the most serious:

Absolute discharge

An absolute discharge means that no penalty at all is imposed upon the offender, and they are not recorded as having a criminal conviction. Section 79 of the SA 20[10] empowers a court to order an absolute discharge providing the case is not one to which any of the provisions specified in s.399 apply; an offence for which the sentence is fixed by law, or an offence for which a mandatory minimum sentence provision applies, and the sentencer does not view the test for disapplication as satisfied.[11]

---

7 An 'either way' offence is one that can be tried by the Magistrates' Court or the Crown Court, and which court hears it will depend on the facts of the case and, to some extent, the choice of the defendant. Even where the prosecution say the matter is suitable for summary trial in the Magistrates' Court, the defendant always has the right with triable either way offences to elect Crown Court trial.

8 S.133(2) of the Magistrates' Courts Act 1980.

9 Murder (Abolition of Death Penalty) Act 1965 – see Chapter 2.

10 Formerly s.12(1)(a) of the PCC(S)A 00.

11 These are provisions requiring courts to impose mandatory minimum sentences for certain sorts of offences, such as a second possession of an offensive weapon or bladed article offence, or the third domestic burglary; within those provisions is a power to disapply the mandatory minimum in 'the interests of justice' or 'exceptional circumstances'. Section

The reason specified in the legislation as justifying an absolute discharge is where the court decides that having regard to the circumstances, including the nature of the offence and the character of the offender, it is inexpedient to inflict punishment (s.79(3)(a) and (b)).

Where an absolute discharge is given, the victim surcharge does not apply. An absolute discharge is deemed not to be a conviction by s.82(2) SA 20.[12]

Conditional discharge

Section 80 SA 20[13] provides a power to conditionally discharge a defendant in the same circumstances as an absolute discharge. A conditional discharge can last for up to three years from the date of the discharge being given (s.80(5)).

The only condition that can be imposed as part of a conditional discharge is that no further offences are committed during the period of the conditional discharge (s.80(1)).

If the defendant ('D') commits any further offences within the period of the conditional discharge, they will be sentenced for the new offence (s.81, and Schedule 2), and the conditional discharge will cease to have effect (s.82(3)). They can also be resentenced for the offence for which the conditional discharge was imposed, to any sentence that would have been available to the court that sentenced the defendant to the conditional discharge (paras. 5–7, Schedule 2).

As with absolute discharges, a conditional discharge is not a conviction (s.82(2)).

Fine

A fine is a monetary penalty paid to the state. The amount of the fine is determined by which 'band' the fine falls into, which determines what proportion of a person's income the fine should comprise. The higher the band, the greater the proportion of D's income. These bands can be found in Sentencing Guidelines, and are shown in Table 0.1.[14]

As the fine is calculated by reference to relevant weekly income, it is important that a court sentencing D by way of a fine has enquired into D's

---

399 of the SA 20 therefore is the consolidating section for a large number of provisions from different statutes that created this position in respect of specific offences within that originating statute.

12 Formerly s.14(1) PCC(S)A 00.

13 Formerly s.12(1)(b) PCC(S)A 00.

14 Table reproduced from www.sentencingcouncil.org.uk/overarching-guides/crown-court/item/imposition-of-community-and-custodial-sentences/.

Table 0.1 Table showing the respective proportions of relevant weekly income of each fine band

	Starting point	*Range*
Fine Band A	50% of relevant weekly income	25–75% of relevant weekly income
Fine Band B	100% of relevant weekly income	75–125% of relevant weekly income
Fine Band C	150% of relevant weekly income	125–175% of relevant weekly income
Fine Band D	250% of relevant weekly income	200–300% of relevant weekly income
Fine Band E	400% of relevant weekly income	300–500% of relevant weekly income
Fine Band F	600% of relevant weekly income	500–700% of relevant weekly income

financial circumstances. This is usually done by way of an MC100 'means form'[15] being provided to the sentencing court. Indeed, s.124(1) SA 20[16] expressly requires that before fixing the level of any fine, the offender's financial circumstances are explored. Within the limits imposed by D's means, the amount of the fine must reflect the seriousness of the offence (s.125(1) SA 20), and the court must take into account the circumstances of the case including any information they have about D's financial circumstances (s.125(2)).

The three highest bands of fine (Bands D, E, and F) can be imposed in place of a Community Order.[17] This will usually occur where, on the advice of the Probation Service, the court decides that the defendant and the wider public would not benefit from the imposition of a Community Order.

The Magistrates' Court can now impose fines with no upper limit as to value.[18] However, where it is a summary-only offence, the Magistrates' Court must adhere to the standard scale of maximum fines for summary offences in s.122(1) SA 20,[19] which is shown in Table 0.2.

15 Available at https://assets.publishing.service.gov.uk/government/uploads/system/uploads/attachment_data/file/688361/mc100-eng.pdf, and provided in hard copy at most Magistrates' Courts.
16 Formerly s.164(1) CJA 03.
17 www.sentencingcouncil.org.uk/overarching-guides/crown-court/item/imposition-of-community-and-custodial-sentences/.
18 Section 85(1) Legal Aid, Sentencing and Punishment of Offenders Act 2012 removed the £5,000 limit on Magistrates' Court fines.
19 Formerly s.37(2) of the Criminal Justice Act 1982.

Table 0.2 Table showing the maximum amount of each fine level

Level on the scale	Amount of fine
1	£200
2	£500
3	£1,000
4	£2,500
5	Unlimited

Where a statute only refers to punishment being by imposing custody, a level 3 fine can be imposed instead, as permitted by s.119(4) SA 20.[20]

Section 120 SA 20[21] expressly permits a Crown Court to fine any offender who has been convicted on indictment, providing the offence is not one for which the sentence is fixed by law, or one that is imposed as a result of a finding that D was dangerous. This fine can be as well as, or instead of, any other sentence that the court thinks appropriate.

Failure to pay a fine is a serious matter – when imposing a fine, the Crown Court must order a period of imprisonment that will be served if the fine is not paid (a period in default – s.129(3) SA 20[22]). The maximum period in default increases depending upon the level of the fine (s.129(4) SA 20). The Magistrates' Court is only exceptionally empowered to impose a term in default.

Community Order

A Community Order ('CO'), as defined by s.200 SA 20[23] is available where D is over 18, and imprisonment is available to the sentencing court (s.201 SA 20).[24] The custody threshold must not have been passed, but a fine would not properly reflect the seriousness of the offence (s.204 SA 20).[25] A CO is not available for offences where the sentence is fixed by law, or where there are particular stipulations regarding sentence such as mandatory minima (s.202(3),[26] s.399 SA 20).

---

20 Formerly s.34(3) of the Magistrates' Courts Act 1980.

21 Formerly s.163 CJA 03.

22 Formerly s.139(2) PCC(S)A 00.

23 Formerly s.177 CJA 03.

24 Though note para. 13, Schedule 22 SA 20, formerly s.151 CJA 03, which would allow for a CO to be imposed on an offender who, since turning 16, has been fined three or more times on conviction, instead of a further fine.

25 Formerly s.148 CJA 03.

26 Formerly s.150(1) CJA 03.

One or more community requirements must be attached to a CO by the sentencing court. The possible requirements available at the date of writing are found under s.201 SA 20, with further details in parts 1–14 of Schedule 9 to the Act:

- an unpaid work requirement
- a rehabilitation activity requirement
- a programme requirement
- a prohibited activity requirement
- a curfew requirement
- an exclusion requirement
- a residence requirement
- a foreign travel prohibition requirement
- a mental health treatment requirement
- a drug rehabilitation requirement
- an alcohol treatment requirement
- an alcohol abstinence and monitoring requirement
- in a case where the offender is aged under 25, an attendance centre requirement
- an electronic compliance or whereabout monitoring requirement

As can be seen from that list, the possibilities are various, and allow a CO to be tailored to the specific offending needs of D being sentenced. In general, a 'pre-sentence report' ('PSR') will be required by the court before a CO is imposed, to ensure that they know enough about the offender to impose appropriate requirements (s.30(2) and (3) SA 20).[27] Such a report is not mandatory however (s.30(4)). Section 44 of the Crime and Courts Act 2013 introduced a requirement that every CO had to contain at least one requirement for the purpose of punishment, unless to do so would be 'unjust in all the circumstances'.[28]

If a CO is not complied with without reasonable excuse, the offender must be given a warning (s.218 and para. 6, Schedule 10, SA 20).[29] If there is a second non-compliance without reasonable excuse within 12 months, the offender must be referred to an enforcement officer. Where the offender is then brought before a court for breach, if the breach is accepted, or proven to the criminal standard, the court must deal with the offender in one of

---

27 Formerly s.156(3) CJA 03.
28 The author has argued elsewhere that this is not a desirable change. See Freer, E. (2017) Punishment and rehabilitation – Uneasy bedfellows under section 44 of the Crime and Courts Act 2013, *Australian and New Zealand Journal of Criminology*, 50(3), pp. 439–455.
29 Formerly para. 5, Schedule 8, CJA 03.

the ways set out in para. 10 (where the case is in the Magistrates' Court), or para. 11 (where it is in the Crown Court), of Schedule 10 to the SA 20, which gives powers summarised as follows:

1   by ordering the offender to pay a fine of £2,500 or less
2   by amending the terms of the Community Order to impose more oner-ous requirements which the sentencing court could include if it were making the CO now
3   resentence D for the original offence in any way the court could have sentenced him for that original offence if he had just been convicted of it
4   where
    (i) the CO was made by a Magistrates' Court,
    (ii) the original offence in respect of which the order was made was not punishable by imprisonment,
    (iii) the offender is aged 18 or over, and
    (iv) the offender has wilfully and persistently failed to comply with the requirements of the order
    by dealing with him, in respect of the original offence, by imposing a sentence of imprisonment for a term not exceeding 51 weeks.

Custody

A custodial sentence is defined by s.222 SA 20[30] as a sentence of imprison-ment (for an adult) or a sentence of detention in youth custody (for a person under 21 at the date of sentencing – s.227[31]).

The maximum custodial sentence for an offence can usually be found in the statute that created the offence. If the statute is silent, and the offence is not one for which a specified or life sentence is stipulated by any enact-ment, then the maximum is two years' custody (s.223 SA 20).[32] Common law offences (such as conspiracy to defraud) are not subject to that limit, but many common law offences now have Sentencing Guidelines which must be applied (see more below on the use of Sentencing Guidelines).

The Magistrates' Court may not impose a sentence of less than five days (s.132 MCA 1980, as per s.229(2)(a) SA 20) or longer than six months for a single offence (s.224(1) SA 20).[33] The Crown Court is lim-ited only by the statutory maximum for the relevant offence. Any court,

---

30 Formerly s.76(1) PCC(S)A 00.
31 Formerly s.89(1) PCC(S)A 00.
32 Formerly s.77 PCC(S)A 00.
33 Formerly s.78(1) PCC(S)A 00.

however, must only use custody of any length as a last resort – s.230(2) SA 20[34] states that a custodial sentence may only be imposed where the court's opinion is that the offence, or it together with another associated offence, is so serious that neither a fine alone nor a community sentence can be justified.

Suspended Sentence Order

Courts have a power to impose these by virtue of s.277 SA 20.[35] A suspended sentence is expressed as a period of imprisonment (between 14 days and 24 months), suspended for a period specified in the order (of between 6 and 24 months – s.288(2)). Some may argue that the Suspended Sentence Order ('SSO') should sit between a Community Order and custody on a hierarchy of seriousness of sentences. There would be sound argument for saying this – it is a period of imprisonment that will not be served within a prison unless the defendant breaches the requirements of the order or commits another offence. However, I have chosen to put SSOs as a subset of custody for a very simple reason.

The first decision that must be taken by a sentencer is whether the custody threshold is crossed. If it is, the sentencer must then calculate what the appropriate sentence would be. Only if that sentence is between 14 days and 24 months, does the possibility of suspension arise. Where the sentence is between 14 days and 24 months, the Judge then has a discretion, guided by a Sentence Guideline,[36] on whether to suspend the sentence. It should be noted that the operation of this discretion does not usually relate to the facts of the offence, but the particular circumstances or attributes of the defendant, as can be seen in the Sentencing Guidelines for the Imposition of Community and Custodial Sentences.[37] The factors explicitly referenced in that Guideline are three in favour of an SSO, and three against.

The three in favour are: a realistic prospect of rehabilitation, strong personal mitigation, and that immediate custody will result in significant harmful impact upon others. The three factors to influence a Judge's discretion

---

34 Formerly s.152(2) CJA 03.

35 Formerly s.189(1) CJA 03.

36 www.sentencingcouncil.org.uk/overarching-guides/crown-court/item/imposition-of-community-and-custodial-sentences/ [accessed 25th November 2020].

37 Crown Court: www.sentencingcouncil.org.uk/overarching-guides/crown-court/item/imposition-of-community-and-custodial-sentences/; Magistrates' Court: www.sentencing council.org.uk/overarching-guides/magistrates-court/item/imposition-of-community-and-custodial-sentences/.

away from suspension and towards an immediate custodial sentence are: offender presents a risk/danger to the public, appropriate punishment can only be achieved by immediate custody, and history of poor compliance with court orders.

An SSO may be 'pure', with no requirements attached, or it may have one or more of the community requirements set out in s.287 SA 20[38] (s.286(2)).[39] If an SSO has no requirements attached, a defendant is only liable to serve the suspended period in custody if they commit another offence during the operational period of the sentence (s.286(1)(a) and (3)).[40] So, for example, a 12-month custodial sentence suspended for 12 months would mean that if D offended again within 12 months of the sentence, they would be taken before the court for breach, and the court would deal with them in one of the ways set out in paragraph 13 of Schedule 16 of the SA 20. The same consequences follow where an SSO has requirements attached and any of the requirements are breached or not undertaken.

If D does breach their SSO by failure to comply with a requirement without reasonable excuse,[41] the responsible officer must give a warning. However, if D has already had one such warning within the previous 12 months, then the responsible officer must refer the matter directly to an enforcement officer.[42] Where there is a further failure to comply with requirements after a warning, or the commission of a further offence, D must be brought back before the court that imposed the suspended sentence, unless it was an SSO made by the Crown Court but containing a direction that breaches could be dealt with by the Magistrates' Court (para. 3, Schedule 10). The court then has a variety of ways in which it can deal with the offender for the breach.

The starting point is that the court will activate the sentence – that is, the defendant will be ordered to serve in prison the entirety (para. 14(1) and para. 13(1)(a)) or part (para. 14(1) and para. 13(1)(b)) of the suspended term unless the court decides it would be unjust to do so in view of all the circumstances. The court must include within those circumstances consideration of the matters mentioned in para. 14(2):

(a) the extent to which the offender has complied with any community requirements of the suspended sentence order, and
(b) the facts of the subsequent offence where there has been one.

---

38 Formerly s.190 CJA 03.
39 Formerly s.189(1A) CJA 03.
40 Formerly s.189(1)(a) CJA 03.
41 Para. 6(1) of Schedule 16 to SA 20, formerly para 4(1) of Schedule 12 to the CJA 03.
42 Para. 6(1) of Schedule 16 to SA 20, formerly para 4(1) of Schedule 12 to the CJA 03.

If the court decides that it would be unjust in all the circumstances to activate the sentence in full or in part, the legislation does provide some other options:

- a fine not exceeding £2,500 (para. 13(1)(c))
- extending the operational period, providing the original operational period was less than 24 months, and the total operational period with the extension does not exceed 24 months (para. 13(1)(d)(iii) and para. 13(1)(e), per s.288(2))

If the SSO contained community requirements, then there are two further options:

- impose more onerous community requirements which would have been available when the original order was made (para. 13(1)(d)(i))
- extend the supervision requirement, providing the total is not more than 24 months (s.288(4)), and the total is not longer than the operational period (para. 13(1)(d)(ii), per s.288(4))

A TYPICAL YEAR IN SENTENCING – SOME STATISTICS

The statistics show that in the 12 months ending June 2019,[43] 1.37 million defendants were prosecuted, with an 87% conviction rate.[44] 1,180,560 million were sentenced.[45] 11,466 of those were recorded as 'other disposals', the main component of which is likely to be those on whom hospital orders were imposed under the Mental Health Act ('MHA') 1983.[46]

---

43 Although the most up to date figures at the time of publication would be those up to June 2020, the coronavirus pandemic necessitated a nationwide lockdown for the final three months of the period covered by those figures, leading to an inaccurate picture. The lockdown caused the closure of all courts and the suspension of all trials in both the Magistrates' and the Crown Courts from the 23rd March until early May, when a tiny handful of trials began at the Old Bailey. From then onwards, the number of jury trials gradually increased.

44 The number of offenders convicted as a proportion of the number prosecuted in a given year.

45 Ministry of Justice (2019) Criminal Justice Statistics, year ending June 2019, London: Ministry of Justice, at p. 4, and Table Q5.1a.

46 Where someone convicted of a crime has a treatable psychiatric illness, under certain circumstances a court can commit them to hospital for treatment. A hospital order (s.37 MHA 1983) is made either with or without a restriction order (s.41). A restriction order is imposed where the defendant is thought to pose a risk of serious harm to the public, and means that they can only be released from the hospital after certain steps have been taken, such as consulting the Secretary of State.

There are a variety of possible sentences as set out above – everything from an absolute discharge to a lengthy period of imprisonment, with conditional discharges, fines, Community Orders, and Suspended Sentence Orders in between. Fines are the most common form of punishment.

In the 12 months to the end of June 2019, fines made up 78% of all sentences,[47] an increase of 12 percentage points since 2009, and a raw number of 916,974.[48] This is in part due to the increasing proportion of sentences for summary offences (83%, a 7 percentage point increase since 2009). Although the sentencing exercises that make the news are invariably those resulting in long periods of imprisonment with tragic and compelling stories behind them, the majority of offenders who are sentenced stand to be sentenced for relatively low-level criminality, in the Magistrates' Court, hence the high proportion of fines.

Meanwhile, there were 38,246 conditional discharges and 4,228 absolute discharges. 90,663 offenders received Community Orders, and 39,200 Suspended Sentence Orders.

The number of offenders sentenced to immediate custody has followed a downward trend since 2016 and decreased 8% to 75,769 in the year ending June 2019. The average custodial sentence length (ACSL) was 17.4 months – showing an increase every year since 2009, when it was 13.5 months. However, there was a reduction of the number of cases in each custodial sentence length category, except life sentences which saw a 20% increase to 459. The number of sentences of a month or less fell by 19% to 10,100. Of all persons sentenced to immediate custody, over half (56%) were sentenced to six months or less. The number of suspended sentences decreased by 19% to 39,200, and community sentences decreased by 1% to 90,600.

Relevant legislation

The process of sentencing is increasingly formulaic. That is in large part because of the increasing amount of legislation prescribing how sentencing should be done. As of 1st December 2020, when the Sentencing Act 2020 came into force, this can now all be found in one place. This is a welcome relief from the myriad number of statutes previously containing sentencing provisions. The section that underpins all sentencing exercises, however, is s.57(2) of the Sentencing Act – formerly s.142 of the Criminal Justice Act 2003.

---

47 Fn 45, at p. 6.
48 Raw numbers taken from Table Q1.5a, Ministry of Justice, 2019.

Section 57 of the Sentencing Act 2020

Section 57(2) provides the five aims of sentencing. The structure of this book follows the structure of section 57, considering each of the five aims, and how we see them brought to life in real sentencing exercises; what they mean for offenders; what theoretical bases they have; and how they have been given force in other jurisdictions.

Section 57 is entitled 'Purposes of sentencing: adults' and subsection 2 reads as follows:

(2) Any court dealing with an offender in respect of his offence must have regard to the following purposes of sentencing –

(a) the punishment of offenders,
(b) the reduction of crime (including its reduction by deterrence),
(c) the reform and rehabilitation of offenders,
(d) the protection of the public, and
(e) the making of reparation by offenders to persons affected by their offences.

Section 57(3) clarifies that these purposes do not apply where there is a mandatory sentence requirement under s.399, or a disposal under Part 3 of the Mental Health Act 1983 (a hospital order, with or without restriction; an interim hospital order; a hospital direction; or a limitation direction). Hospital orders are a disposal available only on the basis of clinical medical evidence.

The role of mandatory minimum sentences is considered throughout this book when looking at punishment and protection. Hospital orders, as a specialist disposal, are not covered.

Applying section 57

When sentencing offenders over the age of 18, however, the court must have regard to section 57. In section 57(1), the first aspect of note is its mandatory and universal application – 'a court' (s.57(1)(a)) dealing with an offender in respect of their offence 'must' have regard to the five purposes listed (s.57(2)). Throughout this book, we see that 'regard' can be shown in many different ways; sometimes expressly, other times implicitly, and demonstrated in the Judge's overall sentencing remarks, and indeed the final sentence.

Sentencing Guidelines

However, many sentencing exercises are shaped by the Sentencing Guidelines for the offence. Guidelines do not exist for all offences, though the number is increasing, as the Sentencing Council continues to update existing guidelines and issue new ones.[49] Due to their increasing significance, a brief history of Sentencing Guidelines in this jurisdiction, and how they are made, is worth considering.

A brief history

Beginning in the 1980s, the Court of Appeal often gave guidance on how a sentence might be arrived at in different kinds of cases (commonly referred to as 'guideline authorities'). These were necessarily piecemeal – the Court of Appeal needed an appropriate case of an offence for which there was no previous guideline authority. Nonetheless, many very serious offences had guidelines created in this way, including rape[50] and burglary.[51] There were also Court of Appeal-created guidelines on procedural matters, such as time served on remand counting towards the final sentence imposed.[52] It was then decided that the creation of guidelines should be formalised; the Crime and Disorder Act 1998 created the Sentencing Advisory Panel (SAP).[53]

The Sentencing Advisory Panel ('SAP')

The SAP drafted, and consulted on, proposals for guidelines giving suggested sentencing ranges for specific offences, and proposing categories within that overarching range depending on the seriousness of the offence. After a consultation, they provided a report to the Court of Appeal for the Judges' consideration. If the Court wished, they could use it to inform a guideline judgment regarding that offence when a suitable case next arose. The Court of Appeal was not obliged to accept the Panel's recommendations,[54] but in most cases it did so,[55] sometimes with the Court making its own modifications.

---

49 www.sentencingcouncil.org.uk.

50 E.g. *Roberts and Roberts* [1982] 4 Cr App R (S) 8.

51 *Brewster* [1998] 1 Cr. App. R. 220.

52 *Oosthuizen* [2005] EWCA Crim 2532 – although by the time that case had reached its appeal hearing, section 240 of the Criminal Justice Act 2003 had enacted that same procedure.

53 Section 81 of the Crime and Disorder Act 1998.

54 For example, in *Poulton* [2002] EWCA Crim 2487 the Court 'largely, though not entirely' adopted the SAP's advice from a report two years earlier (at [19]).

55 The Court considered the SAP's advice in relation to rape, and followed it without deviation, in *Millberry* [2002] EWCA Crim 2891.

However, as each constitution of the Court differed, and the ways in which concepts were expressed therefore varied, this method of giving guidance was not without its difficulties.[56]

In 2001, the Halliday Report recommended that new structures were required to move towards comprehensive Sentencing Guidelines.[57] The Report considered three possible options,[58] and the recommended preferred option – 'Option B' – inspired the creation of the Sentencing Guidelines Council ('SGC').

Therefore, the statutory footing for the SAP was altered in 2004 by s.169 of the Criminal Justice Act 2003. Its new role was to suggest to the SGC areas where guidelines could usefully be created. As section 171(2) provided:

> The Panel may at any time propose to the Council –
>
> a. that sentencing guidelines be framed or revised by the Council –
>
>   (i) in respect of offences or offenders of a particular category, or
>   (ii) in respect of a particular matter affecting sentencing, or
>
> b. that allocation guidelines be framed or revised by the Council.

The SAP consequently continued to draft and consult on Guidelines but the SGC, rather than the Court of Appeal, took ultimate responsibility for the drafting of all Guidelines issued. This was the first time Sentencing Guidelines had been created outside of a court.

The Sentencing Guidelines Council ('SGC')

As well as altering the SAP's remit, s.167 of the Criminal Justice Act 2003 created the Sentencing Guidelines Council – a body headed by the Lord Chief Justice,[59] with seven judicial members[60] and four non-judicial members.[61] Its function was to formulate and draft Sentencing Guidelines based on advice from the SAP.

---

56 See, for example, *Saw* [2009] EWCA Crim 1, clarifying *McInerney and Keating* [2003] which had been subject to some misinterpretation.

57 Halliday, J. (2001) Making Punishments Work: Report Of A Review Of The Sentencing Framework For England And Wales, Chapter 8, p. 54, available at https://webarchive. nationalarchives.gov.uk/ and www.homeoffice.gov.uk/documents/halliday-report-sppu/ [accessed 5th December 2019].

58 *Ibid*, at pp. 53–57.

59 Section 167(1)(a).

60 Section 167(1)(b), further detail given in s.167(2).

61 Section 167(1)(c), further detail given in s.167(4).

Alongside the creation of the SGC was the implementation of legislation to ensure that courts did not simply ignore the resulting guidelines. By s.172(1) of the Criminal Justice Act 2003, any sentencing court had to 'have regard to' any definitive SGC guidelines:

> (1) Every court must –
>
> a. in sentencing an offender, have regard to any guidelines which are relevant to the offender's case, and
> b. in exercising any other function relating to the sentencing of offenders, have regard to any guidelines which are relevant to the exercise of the function.
> (2) In subsection (1) 'guidelines' means sentencing guidelines issued by the Council under section 170(9) as definitive guidelines, as revised by subsequent guidelines so issued.

This applied from February 2004 until April 2010. In April 2010, the Coroners and Justice Act 2009 ('CAJA 09') came into force, bringing with it an even stronger requirement. Under s.125 CAJA 09, now s.59(1) of the Sentencing Act 2020, it is no longer sufficient to 'have regard'. Now, a sentencing court is mandated to follow guidelines unless it can justify a departure. This change is discussed in more detail below.

The Sentencing Council ('SC')

Also in CAJA 09 there was a fundamental change in the structure of the statutory bodies which advised on and issued Sentencing Guidelines. By virtue of s.118 and Schedule 15, both the SGC and the SAP were abolished. In their place was created one unified body, the Sentencing Council ('SC').

Various provisions relating to the constitution and operation of the SC can be found within CAJA 09 in sections 120 to 124. These include the power to make guidelines on any matters,[62] but a mandate to provide guidelines on the reduction for a guilty plea,[63] and on totality.[64] Guidance on the form of factors to be used when considering whether an offender moves up or down within a sentencing range is also included.[65]

---

62 Section 120(4).
63 Section 120(3)(a).
64 Section 120(3)(b).
65 Section 121.

Offences without guidelines

The Court of Appeal is keenly aware of this history of sentencing guidance. In July 2019, it referred to the role of the Sentencing Advisory Panel and its successors.[66] Not every offence is covered by Sentencing Guidelines, and so there remains a role for guideline authorities, albeit a gradually decreasing one. In *Ali and Ors*, the Court of Appeal utilised a previous case informing their view on an appeal against sentence, albeit acknowledging that that judgment was 'not a guideline case in the strict sense'.[67]

A move from guidelines to tramlines?

When Sentencing Guidelines were initially introduced, there was some disquiet amongst the judiciary, used to greater discretion in sentencing, which increased as it produced more guidelines. Some argued that the Sentencing Council was increasing sentence length,[68] something denied by the then-head of the organisation.[69] Sentencing had always been viewed as an exercise of judicial discretion, where precedents could usually, with a bit of careful thought and delicate exposition, be avoided if necessary. Reassurance was provided in the guise of the Guidelines being described as exactly that, and not 'tramlines', something that the Court of Appeal has continued to re-iterate.[70] At the time of the CJA 2003, this was a reassurance that could legitimately be given. Whilst the court 'must have regard to' any relevant Sentencing Guidelines (see above), one can show regard by considering, and then dismissing as inappropriate or unhelpful, the relevant Guideline. Section 52 SA 2020 does require reasons to be given for the sentence arrived at,[71] meaning that an explanation for that departure was expected.

The Court of Appeal has been unimpressed by Judges who depart from a definitive Sentencing Guideline without providing justification, even prior to CAJA 09 when the requirement was no stronger than 'have regard to' the relevant guideline. For example, in *R*,[72] the Court made clear its displeasure at this, and its perceived prevalence:[73]

---

66 *Ali, Mashuk and Syed* [2019] EWCA Crim 1263, at [31].

67 *Ibid*, at [34].

68 Padfield, N. (2016) Guidelines Galore, *Crim. L.R.*, 5, pp. 301–302. Prof Padfield has experience of sitting as a Recorder in the criminal courts.

69 Treacy, LJ. (2016) Letter to the Editor, *Crim. L.R.*, 7, pp. 489–490. Treacy LJ was the then Chair of the Sentencing Council.

70 E.g. *Magness* [2019] EWCA Crim 2071, at [17].

71 Formerly s.174 CJA 03.

72 [2008] EWCA Crim 2615.

73 *Ibid*, at [7].

We would, at this stage, observe that for the second time this morning a case is before us in which the sentencing judge departed from those guidelines, ignoring his statutory duty to explain why it was that he chose to depart from those guidelines.

In 2009, as noted above, the requirement to 'have regard to' changed, with the much stronger wording of s.125(1) CAJA 09, which became s.59(1) of the SA 20. This introduced an express duty on Judges to 'impose on (the offender), in accordance with the offence-specific guidelines, a sentence which is within the offence range' (s.60(2) SA 20). Further, where the Guidelines have different seriousness categories, the Judge is under a duty to identify the category best resembling the present case to identify the relevant starting point (s.60(4)(a)), though is under no duty to impose a sentence within that range (s.60(4)(b)). Section 60(5)[74] provides that s.60(4) does not apply if the Judge concludes that none of the categories sufficiently resembles the present case.

Nonetheless, it is clear that applying Sentencing Guidelines is no longer optional. Even having a stated regard to them, and choosing, for good reasons, to depart, will not be enough unless there are circumstances sufficient to make following them 'contrary to the interests of justice'.[75] Furthermore, sufficient explanation must be given for sentencing outside of the Guideline range.[76]

Everyday sentencing in England and Wales

This book, forming as it does part of the New Trajectories in Law series, seeks to examine sentencing from a different angle. Whilst appeals against sentence and under the unduly lenient sentence scheme heard in the Court of Appeal are reported, and often commentated upon in academic journals, only a tiny number of all sentences are considered by the Court of Appeal.

As noted above, the majority of sentences imposed are fines, and are imposed in the Magistrates' Courts. In the Magistrates' Court, sentencing is often done hurriedly, in a long 'list' of cases waiting to be heard. There might be a Pre-Sentence Report ('PSR') done by the Probation Service, having interviewed the defendant at court. In the Magistrates' Courts these reports are often done the same day as the conviction or guilty plea (called a 'stand down report'). Therefore, as opposed to a written report (usual in the

---

74 Formerly s.125(4) CJA 03.
75 *Bigna* [2019] EWCA Crim 1669.
76 *Ibid*, at [17].

Crown Court) many PSRs in the Magistrates' Court are done by a Probation Officer speaking to the court and answering any questions from the bench or Judge. Such reasons as are provided for the sentence are often given perfunctorily, extempore, and consigned to history almost before their final word is spoken (the Magistrates' Court is not a court of record).

The Crown Court represents a middle ground between the often-chaotic world of Magistrates' Court sentencing, and the Court of Appeal, examining sentences in detail purely to ascertain whether they are 'manifestly excessive'. As sentencing in the Crown Court is done by a Judge alone,[77] reasons relating both to the law and the facts are usually given. This is an advantage of the Judge having heard the facts either during the trial, or a summary of them by the prosecution if there has been a guilty plea (whether at the Crown Court or committed for sentence from a plea in the Magistrates' Court) and the matter is proceeding straight to sentence.

Although it is a requirement that Judges abide by s.57 unless it is 'not in the interests of justice to do so', there is no hierarchy between the five aims, and how each aim can be manifested may be perceived differently by different Judges. At its heart, sentencing is a human exercise, albeit one hedged around with Guidelines. Judges are humans, and so are the defendants whom they are sentencing. As well as a necessary legal exercise at the conclusion of a case, sentencing is a communication between the Judge and the defendant. Sometimes it may also, in part, represent a communication between an entire community and the defendant, or the victim and the defendant. By examining 'everyday' first instance sentencing remarks, these aspects can be teased out, and considered.

An overview of the book

This introductory chapter has done a lot of 'heavy lifting' in providing a brief background explanation of the sentencing system in England. The following chapters focus in on the principles underlying sentencing exercises in a variety of first instance cases. By combining academic literature with an analysis of the sentencing remarks in real cases, a greater insight can be gained into how Judges approach sentencing offenders.

By taking the aims from s.57(2) in order, one per chapter, this book seeks to recognise that not only is there no hierarchy within the legislation, but that in many cases their respective degrees of importance vary. Therefore,

---

77 The only exception is where a Circuit Judge or Recorder hears appeals against sentences imposed by the Magistrates' Court is when s/he will sit with two lay magistrates to decide the case.

Chapter 1 begins with 'Sentencing as Punishment'. This is perhaps the most obvious aspect of any sentence, and what many would assume would be the main purpose identified by the public (though even that presumption is often untrue). By examining what punishment actually is, and whether it is a universal construct, we can better appreciate what it means to punish someone. It also considers whether there is any utilitarian imperative to punish.

Chapter 2 moves to sentencing to reduce crime, and as deterrence. This requires an exploration of whether deterrence is effective, despite a strong political affinity for it, and whether punishment is the only possible route to deterrence.

Moving to sentencing as rehabilitation, Chapter 3 considers to what extent criminal sentencing allows for rehabilitation as a purpose of sentencing, especially considering legislative changes placing a strong focus on punishment. Do traditional discourses of 'punishment' obscure the possibility for innovation by the justice system to facilitate rehabilitation?

Sentencing as protection is the focus of Chapter 4, leading to the question 'protection of whom?' Of past victims, possible future victims, the defendant themselves? The most effective protection is likely to flow from the effective use of the other aims to create a sentence that leads to the defendant not offending again – is that a realistic aim? The role of capital punishment as a device for protection of society is considered within this chapter.

The final substantive chapter takes us to the final aim identified by s.57 – sentencing as reparation. This looks at whether the payment of compensation, for example, can truly provide reparation for a crime, and how reparation is sought to be incorporated within sentences such as Community Orders. It also raises the question of whether restorative justice offers a currently under-used mechanism through which reparation may be made, and its success in other jurisdictions.

Concluding thoughts include whether the five aims and objectives of all sentencing exercises are explicitly deployed in first instance, everyday sentencing exercises, or whether their roles are more subtle and nuanced. It is suggested that the non-hierarchical nature of s.57 is actually a key strength of sentencing legislation, by allowing Judges, even within legislation and Guidelines, to partly tailor a sentence to the individual.

1   Sentencing as punishment

> Punishment: The infliction of a penalty or sanction in retribution for an offence or transgression; (also) that which is inflicted as a penalty; a sanction imposed to ensure the application and enforcement of a law.
>
> (Oxford English Dictionary)

> Punishment is not for revenge, but to lessen crime and to reform the criminal
>
> (Elizabeth Fry[1])

Punishment is perhaps the most obvious aspect of any sentence for a criminal offence, and what many might assume would be the main purpose of sentencing identified by the public. But I would suggest that the criminal justice system has adopted an overly simplistic obsession with punishment, driven by politicians' misunderstanding of what the public actually want to happen to those who break the social contract by offending. It is therefore necessary to interrogate what punishment is, and how we enact it. Whilst in England punishment has become analogous in the eyes of many with imprisonment, is that link a necessary one – can punishment be administered by other sentence types? I suggest that the legislature has overlooked that punishment is experienced by different people in different ways, and different sentences will mete out punishment differently, dependent on the recipient. However, that the societal obsession with imprisonment as the 'only' and paradigm punishment, and a reluctance by politicians to depart from this message, has led to high imprisonment rates and high recidivism rates, suggests that punishment can, far from reforming those

---

1 From a note found among her papers; Cresswell, R. E. and Fry, K. (1848) 'Memoir of the Life of Elizabeth Fry'.

DOI: 10.4324/9781003201625-1

convicted of criminal offences, exacerbate the psychological and contextual factors that influenced their criminality in the first place.

What is punishment?

What is punishment? More pertinently, is punishment the same for everyone? We know from being very young that it is not – if as a child 'as a punishment' I am forbidden from having any crisps, whether or not that is a punishment will depend on how I feel about crisps. If I dislike them, it will be no punishment at all. If I like them a lot, it will be a harsher punishment than if I am ambivalent about them, when it will be a mild punishment. But any punishment relating to crisps would be less harsh than a punishment that forbade me to see my family, for example. Meanwhile, for a child who had an unloving, though not abusive, family from whom they wished to be parted, the deprivation would probably not be such a punishment as to a child who had a loving and secure family, whilst still being much worse than not being permitted crisps.

Furthermore, is punishment necessarily the infliction of pain? Many criminologists argue that imprisonment itself, as a deprivation of liberty, is punishment, as opposed to a medium by which punishment in another form is inflicted. Many of those who are critical of the poor conditions in the prison estate point to the vision of the early prison reformers such as John Howard and Elizabeth Fry who focussed on imprisonment as humane containment – the lack of liberty being the punishment of imprisonment. But in modern society the notion of punishment has often come to incorporate notions of pain, actively caused, as opposed to merely the removal of a freedom usually enjoyed in a liberal society. For example, corporal punishment may be seen as a more serious paradigm punishment as it involves the infliction of physical pain, whilst a prison sentence, as a deprivation of liberty, is not universally regarded as a punishment by the public.

Imprisonment as punishment or for punishment?

It is a longstanding debate as to whether the deprivation of liberty caused by imprisonment is punishment, or whether the offender is being deprived of their liberty in prison in order that other punishments are then administered. Even in circumstances where there is no further deprivation intentionally inflicted by the state beyond the loss of liberty, criminologists have recognised that there are pains associated with imprisonment. In Sykes' famous ethnography of the New Jersey State Prison (1958) these were identified as the loss of five things: liberty, desirable goods and services, heterosexual relationships, autonomy, and security. More recent research has identified that pains of imprisonment are no different in England, and have not abated with the passage of half a century.

Indeed, Crewe has suggested that a number of more modern aspects of imprisonment have in fact caused different pains, as opposed to reduced pains.[2] In 2011, he explored the notions of 'tightness, depth and weight' of the prison experience upon male prisoners. The particular aspects of modern imprisonment that were identified as contributing to the pains of imprisonment were indeterminacy, psychological assessment, and self-government.

Furthermore, greater nuance in the investigation of the pains of imprisonment has identified variation dependent upon the gender of the prisoner and the length of sentence that they are serving. For example, Crewe, Hulley, and Wright[3] found that women reported long-term imprisonment as more painful than long-term male prisoners. The specific pains felt by female prisoners were often shaped by abuse experienced prior to imprisonment – for many, the prison regime brought back memories of past traumas.

Generally the poor standard of much of England's prison estate makes it hard to argue that loss of liberty is the only deprivation experienced within. Take, for example, the description by Her Majesty's Chief Inspector of Prisons ('HMCIP') of the failure to improve HMP Nottingham, over three successive (including two pre-warned) visits:[4]

> The prison was last inspected in early January 2018, which was the third full inspection since 2014. In contrast to our usual practice of arriving unannounced, that inspection and the previous one in 2016 were both announced well in advance. Notice of an impending inspection is intended to give an opportunity to a prison to focus on improvement or on completing earlier recommendations. We therefore found it extraordinary that, over the course of those three inspections, the prison had consistently failed to achieve standards that were sufficient in any of our four tests of a healthy prison. […] We could recall only one other occasion when we had judged safety in a prison to be poor following three consecutive inspections.

2 Crewe, B. (2011) Depth, weight, tightness: Revisiting the pains of imprisonment, *Punishment and Society*, 13(5), pp. 509–529.
3 Crewe, B., Hulley, S., and Wright, S. (2017) The Gendered Pains of Life Imprisonment, *The British Journal of Criminology*, 57(6), pp. 1359–1378.
4 HM Inspectorate of Prisons (2020) Report on an unannounced inspection of HMP Nottingham, London: HMIP, at p. 7. www.justiceinspectorates.gov.uk/hmiprisons/wp-cont ent/uploads/sites/4/2020/03/Nottingham-web-2020.pdf [accessed 2nd November 2020].

It is testament to how bad conditions had been for the 798 men at HMP Nottingham[5] that the following paragraph was seen to represent promising progress, largely attributed to the incoming new Governor, appointed in July 2018 – seven months after the disastrous previous inspection report:[6]

> Given the disappointing and indeed troubling history of poor inspections followed by inadequate responses, it was gratifying to find during this latest inspection that there had at long last been some real change at Nottingham. There had been improvements in three of our tests of a healthy prison, and we came away with some confidence that the improvements could be sustained and built upon if the leadership and energy that was now evident could be maintained into the future. In terms of safety, although there was much data that was troubling and levels of violence were still far too high, we felt able to raise our judgement from poor to not sufficiently good. Too many prisoners still felt unsafe, there was still far too much violence and not enough was yet being done to counter it effectively. However, security had now improved and was beginning to have a positive impact. In particular, a body scanner was now being used to very good effect, leading to regular finds of secreted contraband that would not otherwise have been detected.

The facts page of the report illustrated how at least some difficulties might arise. Nearly half of the population was unsentenced.[7] This means that they were either on remand awaiting trial, or on remand after conviction but awaiting sentence. It is recognised that remand is a time of particular uncertainty for prisoners, and is associated with increased risks of harm and anxiety,[8] which can feed into the wider prison population, as despite significant differences in the rules applicable to remand prisoners, they are usually held with the sentenced population – something HMIP advised the National Offender Management Service (NOMS) (now Her Majesty's Prison and Probation Service) should be changed in 2012.[9]

---

5 *Ibid*, at p. 9.
6 *Ibid*, at p. 7.
7 Section 57 considerations are not relevant to a decision to remand in custody pending trial or sentence; that decision is taken on the basis of Schedule 1 to the Bail Act 1976 prior to a conviction, and after conviction is purely a matter of judicial discretion. This book does not cover bail and remand.
8 Her Majesty's Inspectorate of Prisons (2012) *Remand prisoners: A thematic review*, London: HM Inspectorate of Prisons, pp. 7–9. www.justiceinspectorates.gov.uk/hmiprisons/wp-cont ent/uploads/sites/4/2012/08/remand-thematic.pdf [accessed 2nd November 2020].
9 *Ibid*, p. 17.

60% of prisoners surveyed by the Inspector's team had self-reported mental health problems.[10] Many defendants in the criminal justice system have pre-existing poor mental health, such that the law reform and human rights organisation JUSTICE argued that defendants' fair trial rights were affected, and made 52 recommendations for how the criminal justice system could ensure fair trial rights for those with mental health conditions and learning disabilities. Considering that in 1998 comprehensive data showed that 90% of the prison population had one or more of the five psychiatric disorders studied (psychosis, neurosis, personality disorder, hazardous drinking, and drug dependence),[11] when the identification of mental health conditions was generally less reliable than now, it seems unlikely that that proportion will have dropped significantly. These conditions are all likely to be exacerbated by imprisonment, even where that is not the intention of the state, increasing the intensity of punishment experienced by the prisoner independent of the seriousness of their offending. Variation in the severity of the punishment experienced is dependent upon the attributes of the person to whom it is given, and that demonstrates a challenge of the sentencing mechanism at its most fundamental level, which has led some to argue that 'negotiated sentencing', accounting for such matters, is the way forward.[12]

More basic deprivations were also seen in the inspection of HMP Nottingham. For example:[13]

> Key concern: Prisoners' access to prison clothing, including underwear and bed linen, remained very poor. For example, some prisoners had been wearing the same clothes for a week or more. Recommendation: All prisoners must have regular access to an adequate amount of clean prison clothing and bedding.

Having access to clean clothes is a comfort that many would take for granted, and many would find staying in the same clothing for over a week to be an unpleasant experience akin to further punishment. Even issues such as this lead to questions over whether the way in which the English prison estate is managed and maintained makes imprisonment far more than

---

10 Fn 4, at p. 9.
11 Singleton, N. et al. (1998) Psychiatric morbidity among prisoners in England and Wales, London: Office for National Statistics.
12 Van Ginneken, E. F. J. C. (2016) The pain and purpose of punishment: A subjective perspective, Howard League What is Justice? Working Papers 22/2016, London: The Howard League for Penal Reform, https://howardleague.org/wp-content/uploads/2016/04/HLWP -22-2016.pdf [accessed 2nd November 2020].
13 Fn 4, at p. 21.

punishment by deprivation of liberty, imposing further punishment through substandard living conditions. Whilst I have used the example of HMP Nottingham above, there are many reports of the HMCIP which rehearse similarly dreadful conditions at many other English prisons.[14]

Are imprisonment and incapacitation synonymous?

One theory of punishment is incapacitation. It has a very simple premise – that if someone is incapacitated, they are unable to act as they wish. In so doing, they are theoretically both punished, and prevented from committing further offences (see Chapter 2). There are, however, two challenges to that notion. Firstly, prisoners can, and do, commit crimes whilst in prison against both other prisoners and staff, including homicide.[15] Secondly, degrees of incapacitation can be imposed without the need for imprisonment, such as by a curfew, which is available as a community requirement attached to COs and SSOs.

For example, when sentencing MM for drink-driving, the magistrates imposed a curfew in tandem with a Rehabilitation Activity Requirement ('RAR'), illustrating the capacity for a sentencing option based in the community that could nonetheless combine an element of incapacitation for punishment with an element of rehabilitation to support MM in addressing the circumstances leading to her offending:[16]

> To be driving with that amount of alcohol in your system at that time with intention of picking your boys up from school [was totally unacceptable]. [We are] going to look at the Community Order that we're going to instigate. We're not considering custody and we're not going to give a suspended sentence. We're giving you a high-level community order. For the offence of driving a motor vehicle when alcohol above the legal limit was sufficient for us to make a high-level Community Order. This order will last for 12 months. [...] We understand you are not suitable for an Alcohol Treatment Requirement[17] but RAR days will address various aspects of your offending behaviour including why you drank to excess on that day and how your other health issues

---

14 All are available on Her Majesty's Chief Inspector of Prisons' website: www.justiceinsp ectorates.gov.uk/hmiprisons/#.U4yR31Mumjg [accessed 1st November 2020].

15 Freer, E. (2012) University of Cambridge, unpublished Masters' thesis.

16 *R v MM*, Cambridge Magistrates' Court, 19th July 2019.

17 The Probation Officer who had interviewed MM had noted that her having consumed a large amount of alcohol on this particular occasion was not part of an established behaviour pattern requiring an ATR.

impact each other. We are going to impose a curfew. It ends at 6am so that if you are looking for cleaning jobs they often start early and so you might be able to work.

Whilst a curfew imposes a physical incapacitation by restricting the offender to a registered address between specified hours over a relatively few weeks, there are other ways in which a partial incapacitation may be imposed. For example, where an offence leads to a disqualification from driving, the offender may feel that that is an incapacitation of sorts, especially if their day-to-day activities will be curtailed without access to a car. That incapacitation is likely to be greater if they do not live in an area well-connected by public transport. Whilst these matters should be considered by the court when passing sentence, and adjustments can, within reason, be made to the length of disqualification as a result, avoiding disqualification where the offender has committed a serious offence of speeding is extremely difficult. If the offender was drink- or drug-driving then the disqualification is mandatory (unless they successfully advance 'special reasons').[18]

When fining EA for a speeding offence,[19] the magistrates observed that there had to be a disqualification, but did not address whether this was punitive, or protective of the public from the dangers created by driving at outrageous speeds:

> We have listened to all the things said. We accept this was a one-off and you were in a different vehicle. However 120mph is not acceptable. Looking at the guidelines and you're out of the box [of the top sentencing bracket]. You don't even fit in the requirements. We're going to disqualify you from driving for 30 days. We hope you've got some holiday for your job. 120mph needs a disqualification. It's not anything else.

In that defendant's situation, the incapacitation of not being able to drive was going to mean he could not go to work unless he found a colleague who was willing to drive out of their way to pick him up, hence the reference from the magistrate about hoping the defendant had some holiday from his job that he could use to span some of the period of the disqualification. For someone who lives in central London, where the transport links are very good, often available 24 hours, and include choice about mode of travel (i.e. bus, Tube, train), the incapacitation experienced as a result of a disqualification from driving would be likely to be significantly less.

18 Road Traffic Offenders Act 1988, s.34(1).
19 *R v EA*, Ipswich Magistrates' Court, 14th February 2018.

This raises an important point about sentencing that can lead to criticism – that it necessarily assumes that each person will experience a certain sentence type/length in broadly the same way. This, of course, is contrary to human nature.

Punishment as universal construct

The criminal justice system proceeds broadly on the basis that punishment is a universal construct. It assumes that any person will experience more 'punishment' from a custodial sentence than a community order ('CO'), and from a community order than from a fine. The common-sense conclusion, supported by research,[20] is that this is not correct. If a person has almost no money at all, and is reluctantly unemployed, a fine, even adjusted by their circumstances, might feel more punitive to them than a CO with a short period of unpaid work, which would cost them nothing and give them a short-term purpose. Similarly, some offenders say that they find a prison sentence 'easier' than a CO or an SSO with requirements attached, as it just requires them to wait out their time in prison, as opposed to actively engage in a programme or keep commitments, on pain of imprisonment for breach if they do not do so:[21]

> Several indicated that community sentences were harder to complete than a short prison sentence because of the need to keep to appointments and the length of time over which community sentences are completed. Some highlighted that it was hard to comply with community sentences because they had to manage their day-to-day lives and the factors that had often led them to offend (most commonly drug use).

COs and SSOs were sometimes perceived by the public as a 'soft option';[22] in 2010 a survey showed that 38% of a survey group said the phrase 'a soft option' best described 'community sentences'. 22% said they were 'weak and undemanding'.[23] Magistrates had a more nuanced view – a 2008 survey by the

---

20 For example, van Ginneken, E. F. J. C. and Hayes, D. (2017) 'Just' punishment? Offenders' views on the meaning and severity of punishment, *Criminology and Criminal Justice*, 17(1), pp. 62–78.

21 Trebilcock, J. (2011) No winners: The reality of short term prison sentences, London: The Howard League for Penal Reform.

22 Kaye, R. (2010) Fitting the Crime – Reforming community sentences: Mending the weak link in the sentencing chain, London: Policy Exchange. www.policyexchange.org.uk/wp-content/uploads/2016/09/fitting-the-crime-nov-10.pdf [accessed on 2nd November 2020].

23 *Ibid*, at p. 110 – YouGov/Policy Exchange Poll; total sample size 2,082 adults surveyed online on 16th and 17th November 2010. The figures were weighted and are representative of all Great British adults (aged 18 and over).

Probation Service found that almost 50% of magistrates agreed that community sentences were a 'soft option'. However, more than 75% of magistrates agreed that community sentences are 'a punishment for offenders'.[24] Meanwhile, victims of offences also expressed concerns that community sentences (in that study, exclusively COs) were not taken seriously by offenders, and that where they were not taken seriously there were not sufficient consequences.[25]

Despite the view expressed in research literature, such as that cited above, that offenders viewed community sentences as anything but easy, it was decided that community disposals needed 'toughening up'. The 'solution' to this perceived problem was implemented through s.44 of the Crime and Courts Act 2013. This required that any CO contain a requirement which had the purpose of punishment, such as a fine, a curfew, or an unpaid work requirement, unless there were exceptional circumstances. Purely rehabilitative COs were therefore no longer permitted, unless there was an 'exceptional circumstance'.

In other words, a sentence that does not incorporate punishment must be an exceptional thing.[26] Yet this rhetoric fails to acknowledge the huge variety in offenders and offences within the criminal justice system. For example, it is in tension with research showing the huge number of defendants with mental health problems,[27] which for many of whom are linked in some way with their offending, and could be helped by 'pure' rehabilitation.

For this reason alone, it is difficult to imagine that every offender whose offending stems from matters that could be helped by rehabilitation could be classed as having 'exceptional circumstances' considering the prevalence of offending that stems from drug and alcohol dependency and mental health problems.[28] Meanwhile, no punitive element has to be added to SSOs because the fact that it is a custodial sentence fulfils the punitive aspect. Therefore, it is open to a sentencer to make a 'pure' SSO (as described in the Introduction).

Relevant to the discussion about how offenders generally experience community sentences is that the criminal justice system proceeds on the

---

24 MORI/Home Office (2008) Magistrates' perceptions of the Probation Service, London: MORI, at p. 18, quoted by *ibid*, at p. 38.

25 Victim Support and Make Justice Work (2012) Out in the open: What victims really think about community sentencing, London: Victim Support. www.victimsupport.org.uk/sites/default/files/Out%20in%20the%20open%20-%20what%20victims%20really%20think%20about%20community%20sentencing.pdf [accessed 2nd November 2020].

26 Freer, E. (2017) Punishment and rehabilitation – Uneasy bedfellows under section 44 of the Crime and Courts Act 2013, *Australian and New Zealand Journal of Criminology*, 50(3), pp. 439–455.

27 E.g. Durcan, G. (2016) Mental health and criminal justice: A view from consultations across England and Wales, Centre for Mental Health, pp. 7–8.

28 *Ibid*.

basis that certain characteristics entitle someone to a lesser sentence. The most common of these are being a first time offender, and pleading guilty to the offence. Other, less common, reasons include assisting the prosecution, for example, under s.73 of the Serious Organised Crime and Police Act 2005. A closer examination of these factors reveals some implicit assumptions on behalf of the legislature.

First-time offenders

Those of 'previous good character' (i.e. without any cautions or convictions prior to the matter for which the court is sentencing them) benefit from their lack of previous convictions when being sentenced.

Although some refer to a 'first time offender discount', it is in fact the opposite – those with previous convictions see their sentence aggravated because of their previous convictions. This is enshrined in statute, with s.65(2) of the SA 20[29] reading as follows:

> In considering the seriousness of an offence ('the current offence') committed by an offender who has one or more previous convictions, the court must treat each previous conviction as an aggravating factor if (in the case of that conviction) the court considers that it can reasonably be so treated having regard, in particular, to –
>
> (a) the nature of the offence to which the conviction relates and its relevance to the current offence, and
> (b) the time that has elapsed since the conviction.

Therefore there is a sliding scale – the less relevant and the longer ago the conviction(s) were, the less effect they will have on the sentence passed. If they are not relevant then they cannot be taken into account at all. There are various theoretical justifications advanced for this – including that the offender's culpability is lower as, having had not any prior contact with the criminal justice system, they did not fully understand what they were doing.[30] Alternatively, some say that the 'reduction' reflects that a first time offender, unlike a repeat offender, has not previously experienced the censure of the criminal justice system and failed to respond to it.[31] A third

---

29 Formerly s.143(2) of the CJA 03.
30 Roberts, J. V. (2009) 'Revisiting the Recidivist Sentencing Premium' in A. von Hirsch, A. Ashworth, and J. V. Roberts (eds), Principled Sentencing: Readings on Theory and Policy, 3rd ed, Oxford: Hart Publishing, p. 150.
31 *Ibid*, and also Lee, Y. (2009) Recidivism as Omission: A Relational Account (2009) 87 *Texas Law Review*, p. 571.

alternative suggested is that the first time offender can sensibly argue that the offence was merely a lapse – a departure from their usual behaviour[32] – though understandable doubt has been displayed as to whether this can be properly applied to all offences, such as those that are extremely serious.[33] For some offences, such as murder, their severity means that previous good character will contribute less than in lower-level offending.

Nonetheless, the overall effect is that defendants receive recognition of their previous good character when the Judge is setting the type and/ or length of the sentence to be imposed. For some defendants, their good character is something they have had for a very long time, as recognised by the Judge sentencing WS for having indecent images of children on his computer:[34]

> It is sad to see you at the age of 73, a man of good character, coming before the criminal court; Crown Court no less, on such serious matters, and you should be ashamed of yourself for allowing that to happen.

For those of good character insofar as having no criminal convictions, there may be aspects of their behaviour, of which the Judge is aware, that means they will not receive the full reduction available to someone whose previous conduct had been wholly blameless.[35] For example, in sentencing TC for offences related to his business, when there was evidence that he had also behaved without propriety (though not criminally) in relation to a business that he had previously run, the Judge said:[36]

> He is not in good character except in the technical sense of having no previous convictions or cautions – his behaviour regarding [a previous company] puts him outside that in the view of any right-minded person.

Pleading guilty

Defendants who plead guilty save the criminal justice system vast amounts of time and money. It is therefore perhaps unsurprising that the system

---

32 von Hirsch, A. (1981) Desert and Previous Convictions, *Minnesota Law Review*, 65, p. 591.
33 Ryberg, J. (2010) 'Recidivism, Retributivism, and the Lapse Theory of Previous Convictions' in J. V. Roberts (ed.), Previous Convictions at Sentencing: Theoretical and Applied Perspectives, Oxford: Hart Publishing, at p. 39.
34 *R v WS*, Luton Crown Court, 6th April 2018.
35 For example, as per *Mitchell*, where there were previous incidents that had not led to criminal justice intervention: [2016] UKSC 55.
36 *R v TC*, Maidstone Crown Court, 12th December 2018.

'rewards' a guilty plea by a reduction in sentence mandated by a specific Sentencing Guideline.[37] For example, SN,[38] being sentenced for drink-driving, was told by the magistrates:

> You said yourself this was a bad decision. And you know that now. You have pleaded guilty so we punish you a little bit less. We have considered that and taken that into account. We are going to order that you pay a fine of £250. We have reached that because we have listened to what you have said about how much money you have and we have lowered it because you have pleaded guilty.

For MM,[39] also being sentenced for drink driving, a combination of her guilty plea and her previous good character took her below the custody threshold:

> This offence crossed the custody threshold, but due to you having no previous convictions and your guilty plea, we have brought that down.

Although it is not permitted for a Judge to increase the sentence because a defendant did not plead guilty and is convicted at trial, it is not unknown for Judges to express their frustration when defendants who could not run a positive defence nonetheless contest a trial by 'putting the Crown to proof',[40] as SP did in a trial for possession of Class A drugs with intent to supply:[41]

> You must have been told that you can't run a positive case but you decided to plead not guilty. The jury saw through that non-existent defence. I don't sentence you to any longer term [because you had a trial], but you do not get the credit you should have had for pleading guilty.

Personal attributes

The variation between offenders' experiences of punishment based on personal characteristics is increasingly recognised. For example, Shona

37 Sentencing Council [2017] Overarching Guideline: Reduction in Sentence for Guilty Plea, London: Sentencing Council, www.sentencingcouncil.org.uk/publications/item/reduction-in-sentence-for-a-guilty-plea-definitive-guideline-2/ [accessed 1st November 2020].
38 *R v SN*, Oxford Magistrates' Court, 16th March 2017.
39 *R v MM*, Cambridge Magistrates' Court, 19th July 2019.
40 This referring to a defendant who does not advance a positive case that they did not commit the offence, but instead seeks to undermine the prosecution's evidence through cross-examination of witnesses, in the hope that the tribunal of fact will not be 'sure' (the standard of proof for criminal convictions in England and Wales) that the defendant committed the offence, and will thus acquit them.
41 *R v SP*, Southwark Crown Court, 22nd February 2018.

Minson's research into the effect of imprisonment of mothers on both them and their children[42] led to an expanded explanation for the mitigating factor 'sole or primary carer for dependent relatives' in the Sentencing Guideline on Overarching Principles, assisting sentencers on how to consider the effects of parental imprisonment upon dependent children when sentencing primary carers.[43] It is recognised that the impact of imprisonment of a primary caregiver is unrelated to their sex,[44] and that caregiving responsibilities may not be limited to children, but can include elderly relatives.

An example of a Judge acknowledging the caring responsibilities of a defendant was seen in sentencing FA,[45] who had committed benefit fraud by failing to notify the council of a change of circumstances when her husband, who had left, returned to live with her. Even when he had been living elsewhere, he had been paying the mortgage, meaning she did not qualify for the Council Tax relief and Income Support that she had claimed:

> The situation was that it is possible that at times your husband, who was responsible for you and the children, was not with you but the mortgage was being paid and at times he certainly was with you. Despite that you continued to claim these benefits. You are stealing from everybody, at a time when resources are very stretched in this country and you should be ashamed of yourself. You are a woman without any previous convictions, aged 32. You have a family; two small children. This is depressingly familiar. According to the Guidelines for sentencing these offences, your culpability is in Category B, and Harm Category 4. That is a starting point based on £30,000 unlawfully claimed.[46] The starting point is therefore 36 weeks' imprisonment. You're entitled to a third credit for your plea of guilty, reducing the sentence to 6 months. The only question I have is whether it should be immediate or suspended. Much though I think this is becoming a serious problem, I have to have regard to your two children. I do so not for you but for those children. You do not deserve the mercy which I am going to show [in suspending the sentence]. 6 months concurrent on each of these counts, suspended

---

42 See Minson, S. (2019) Direct harms and social consequences: An analysis of the impact of maternal imprisonment on dependent children in England and Wales, *Criminology and Criminal Justice*, 19(5), pp. 519–536; and Minson, S (2019) 'Maternal Sentencing and the Rights of the Child'. Hampshire: Palgrave.

43 See Sentencing Council (2019) General Guideline: Overarching Principles – www.senten cingcouncil.org.uk/overarching-guides/magistrates-court/item/general-guideline-overar ching-principles/ [accessed 21st May 2021].

44 See *Bishop (Wayne Steven)* [2011] EWCA Crim 1446.

45 *R v FA*, Luton Crown Court, 11th August 2017.

46 FA's fraud had a value of £35,624.

for 2 years [...] you will be subject to a curfew 7pm–7am, electronically monitored, for 4 months.

Whilst the attributes of the defendant and their decision to plead guilty early in the criminal proceedings may reduce their sentence, there is a wider question to be asked about whether punishment is as highly desired by the public as many politicians seek to portray it.

Populist punitiveness[47] – is punishment what the public want?

Research suggests that the public's interests are actually more nuanced. In 1996, the British Crime Survey ('BCS' – now named the Crime Survey of England and Wales 'CSEW') contained additional questions to explore how the public viewed sentencers and sentencing.[48] The answers to these questions revealed that 25% of a subsample of 50% (8,365) of the respondents to the 1996 BCS thought that Judges were doing a good job.[49] Only 18% thought that Judges were 'in touch with what ordinary people think'. 79% of the sample thought that sentences were too lenient to some degree, whilst 51% thought that they were much too lenient.[50] The statistically significant relationship between those who thought that Judges were out of touch and those who thought that sentences were much too lenient demonstrated that those people viewed the leniency of sentences as a manifestation of the Judges being out of touch with what ordinary people think.[51]

However, when given even just a specific offence type (so encapsulating all possible factual variations within one offence), the public who participated in the BCS tended to underestimate. They were asked 'for every 100 men aged 21 or over who are convicted of rape/mugging/house burglary, how many do you think are sent to prison?'. In 1995, the correct answer was that 97% of those convicted of rape went to prison. However, only 18% of the BCS participants gave a response that the researchers termed as 'accurate' – that between 85% and 100% of the males convicted of rape went to prison. 12% of the sample gave an 'accurate' (60%–79%) answer

---

47 This term was coined by Anthony Bottoms in 1990 to encompass the perceived desire of the public for harsh sentences for all offenders.
48 See Roberts, J. V. and Hough, M. (1999) Sentencing Trends in Britain: Public Knowledge and Public Opinion, *Punishment and Society*, 1(1), pp. 11–26.
49 *Ibid*, at p. 14.
50 *Ibid*, at p. 15.
51 *Ibid*.

for mugging (defined as street robbery),[52] and 22% for burglary (accurate answers being anywhere between 50%–69%).[53] This illustrated that the public as represented in that sample did not have an accurate perception of whether offenders actually went to prison. Overall, those who were the most pessimistic about crime levels and the appropriateness of sentencing outcomes were also the most likely to say that sentences were 'too soft'.[54]

Respondents were then asked what sentence they thought was appropriate on a set of specific facts, which depicted a 23-year-old who had pleaded guilty to the burglary of the cottage of an elderly man whilst the man was out during the day. A video player worth £150 and a television were stolen, and found damaged near the scene. The offender had previously been convicted of burglary.[55] Only 54% of respondents, having heard the facts, opted for imprisonment. Respondents were more likely to favour imprisonment where they had not been given a list of possible sentencing options, suggesting perhaps that for many people, it is simply the first criminal justice disposal that comes to mind. Community Orders, Suspended Sentence Orders, fines and discharges, meanwhile, may be less well-known. For example, 22% of those who had not seen a list of possible options, as compared to 44% of those who had, selected 'compensation' as appropriate in the burglary case.

This research, although now 20 years old, illustrates the dangers of the common political argument that 'the public want harsher sentences'. Whilst this might be superficially true, and true of some specific demographic groups,[56] it tends not to be accurate when members of the public are presented with specific facts. The importance of accurate press reporting of sentence hearings, both the prosecution opening[57] and the mitigation advanced by the defence, is thus reinforced – the more the public know about an offence, the less likely they are to view the sentence as inappropriate.[58]

It also demonstrates the conflation of punishment with imprisonment. Whilst of course imprisonment is a punishment, our criminal justice system increasingly perceives it as the paradigm punishment. This is exacerbated by news reports that portray even an SSO as 'getting away' with an offence

---

52 *Ibid*, at p. 17.
53 *Ibid*, at pp. 16–17.
54 *Ibid*, at p. 18.
55 *Ibid*, at p. 19.
56 *Ibid*, at p. 18.
57 The prosecution set out the facts of the offence at a sentencing hearing, and also draw the Judge's attention to any relevant Guidelines or other provisions of law that s/he is required to apply. The prosecution does not argue for a sentence of a particular length.
58 Fn 48, at p. 23.

– as the defendant 'escaping custody'.[59] As noted in the Introduction, that is a fundamental mischaracterisation of an SSO,[60] which is a custodial sentence, suspended on condition of no further offences and, in many cases, the imposition of stringent community requirements. As demonstrated throughout this book, Judges consider carefully whether they should activate SSOs when they are breached through further offences. One such example was LW,[61] charged with having an offensive weapon – a belt:

> You are a young man of 19 but you are building up a list of previous convictions, all concerning, more or less, weapons. You have your first conviction for possession of [a] bladed article for which you made subject to a Referral Order. That was in 2010. [...] In 2011 you have a conviction for possession of an offensive weapon, but you were given a supervision requirement and a Youth Rehabilitation Order. In 2013 you came back before the courts for robbery, common assault and drugs. Again you were given a non-custodial sentence. Back for breach in 2014. In November last year (2015) for being in possession of a knife, you were sentenced to an SSO for 6 months wholly suspended for 2 years, so that does not expire until 2017. It had attached 80 hours' unpaid work and a programme requirement and I have seen the report prepared on 8th March requiring an amendment to the rehabilitation activity as there were concerns about you having to attend Southwark to comply.[62] That was done. But of 80 hours ordered you have only completed 10 and a half and had been offered 12 appointments but only complied with 2. You expressed some fear for your own safety but arrangements were made to go to different projects on three separate occasions. Now you are back before the courts for the belt. It was carried because you would use it, if the occasion arose, for your own protection. It was submitted on your behalf not to activate the SSO. It seems to me that the time has come when the courts, having given you chance after chance, you must realise that it is extremely dangerous to carry weapons of any kind in a public place, especially with the intention to use it. This occurred within 6 months of the SSO being imposed and with you not having complied in full or done much to comply with it.

59 Cuthbertson, P. (2014) Suspended Sentences: The Case for Abolition, Centre for Crime Prevention, Research Note 4 https://drive.google.com/file/d/0B25IaOtJKlvwam5mR EhqU3JQUVE/edit [accessed 21st May 2021].
60 See, for example, www.sentencingcouncil.org.uk/blog/post/non-custodial-sentences-wa lking-free-from-court/ [accessed 21st May 2021].
61 *R v LW*, Inner London Crown Court, 25th July 2016.
62 LW was involved in gang activity and was having to enter a rival gang's territory to complete the requirement, prior to the amendment.

I have no choice but to activate at least part of the SSO. I give credit for plea and consider you are only 19 and bear in mind agreement between Prosecutor and Defence that this in lowest category as far as magistrates' court is concerned. But this is a committal for sentence. You're in breach of a Crown Court SSO. According to magistrates' court the starting point if only offence is high level CO with range Band C fine to 12 weeks' custody. Bearing in mind everything submitted on your behalf, and antecedence, I am prepared to accept lowest category. In relation to this matter, least possible sentence is one of 8 weeks in custody. I also activate part of the SSO – I activate 3 months of that order and that will run consecutively to present sentence passed upon you today. So total of 5 months in YOI [Young Offender Institution].

This was an example of an offender who had been given multiple chances to engage with rehabilitative options. Having not fully done so, the Judge felt compelled to activate part of the SSO and impose immediate custody for the new offence.

Utilitarian perspectives – is there an imperative to punish for the greater good?

In considering whether there is any utilitarian imperative to punish, I suggest that the picture is not straightforward. Whilst Classical thinkers supported the idea that transgression of the social contract needed to be met with punishment, a modern approach must consider the greater recognition of the factors that lead to offending. Any portrayal of an offender as 'someone who chooses to break the law' will apply only to a minority of offenders. Part of the inspiration for this book was a client whom I represented in 2017. To avoid identifying him, details will be kept to those in the public domain.[63] It remains a case that has had a significant impact on my understanding of the sometimes complex interplay between the objectives of s.57(2), and the determination to operate only the objectives in s.57 at the sentencing stage of a case. The absence of the opportunity to meaningfully explore objectives such as rehabilitation and deterrence prior to charge, in appropriate cases, can mean that someone is put through the criminal justice when there is no apparent utility to doing so.

OT was a young man of good character.[64] He had had serious mental ill health, successfully controlled by medication, stemming partly from

---

63 The details provided were all recited in open court, and therefore could have been heard and reported by any member of the public or press. Nothing contained in the facts given comes from instructions which were not then used in mitigation in open court.

64 *R v OT*, Stevenage Magistrates' Court, 3rd May 2017.

community hostility towards his sexuality as a teenager. He was a teaching assistant. One of the medications for his mental health reacted extremely strongly with alcohol. One evening OT had consumed alcohol with friends. On his train journey home, OT argued with passenger A; passenger B tried to diffuse this. OT interpreted passenger B as being aggressive. On alighting the train, OT punched passenger B, breaking his nose. OT was charged with assault by beating.[65] When shown the CCTV at the police station, being unable to remember most of the incident, OT wept and offered his apologies to the victim. He pleaded guilty at the first appearance in the magistrates' court.

As explained in the Introduction, it is possible for a court to impose a high level (Band D, E, or F) fine in circumstances where the Community Order (CO) threshold is passed, but there are good reasons why the intervention of the Probation Service is unnecessary.

In OT's case, the magistrates characterised a Community Order as carrying a level of punishment that was 'not appropriate' for OT, and imposed a Band D fine, saying;

> You know all the facts. It is never comfortable to hear it all again. The trouble is, even in an unthought and unprovoked attack; you hit someone hard, and don't realise the damage you can do – serious injury. That's why we've been discussing where it sits [on the Guidelines]. We found greater harm, not planned in any way but the consequence was serious. Because of that, this offence crosses the Community Order threshold – normally that would mean that you would deal with Probation and get punishment but we have heard about your own background, and we think it is not appropriate for you to have one of those punishments, so we are imposing a financial penalty.
>
> You must also pay compensation of £1500 to [victim]. Pay Band D fine of £300 which would have been much more if you had not pleaded guilty at first opportunity.

On leaving the court, OT was approached by a woman who had been sitting in the public gallery.[66] She was the wife of the victim, and told OT emphatically that had her husband known everything said in mitigation, he would have strenuously opposed the police charging OT – all he had wanted was

---

65 Though a broken nose could (and arguably should) have been charged as grievous bodily harm – s.20 Offences Against the Person Act 1861, or at the very least assault occasioning actual bodily harm – s.47 Offences Against the Person Act 1861. Whilst it was good news for OT that he was not charged with anything more serious, it shows a bewildering charging approach by the CPS.

66 This conversation occurred in the public waiting area of the court, hence it not being confidential.

an apology, and was worried that the man who had hit him was danger-ous – an understandable concern where a man had punched a stranger to the head after a minor verbal argument. She was adamant that some kind of process that lawyers would identify as restorative justice (see Chapter 5) would have been more satisfactory for everybody.

Would punishment through a CO have served a purpose with this young man? It cannot be known for sure, but it seemed extremely unlikely. He had voluntarily engaged with counselling and was well-supported. The mag-istrates seemed to adopt the same view. However, the sentence that they imposed upon him, a purely financial one, was still punitive to him, and would be even more so if imposed upon someone of less means. Furthermore, the very act of charging and then sentencing him led to outcomes that for him would be extremely punitive – most notably, their presence on a DBS check,[67] and likely loss of a job to which he was clearly devoted. Arguably this was a young man for whom the 'punishment' had been meted out through being charged and pleading guilty, and their consequences, aside from any sentence.

Indeed, some criminologists have recognised the act of arrest as itself amounting to a criminal sanction.[68] Though the Supreme Court of the United States has ruled that pre-trial detention is not punishment,[69] by 1992, fifteen US states had enacted mandatory arrest laws for misdemeanour domestic battery[70] offences.[71] This demonstrates that mandatory arrest is perceived as a criminal sanction leading to a specific deterrent effect.[72] For those of good character, this feeling of being sanctioned by the arrest itself may be ampli-fied where they are arrested in public or in the presence of family or friends, where the arrest has an effect on future leisure or work travel plans,[73] or where knowledge of it may get back to their employer.[74]

---

67 Disclosure and Barring Service – a DBS check is needed to work with children and vulner-able adults.
68 Sherman L. W.; Schmidt, J. D.; Rogan, D. P.; Smith, D. A.; Gartin, P. R.; Cohn, E. G.; Collins, D. J.; Bacich, A. R. (1992) Variable Effects of Arrest on Criminal Careers: The Milwaukee Domestic Violence Experiment, *Journal of Criminal Law and Criminology*, 83(1), pp. 137–169, at p. 138.
69 *Bell v Wolfish*, 441 U.S. 520 (1979).
70 Lower-level offences than felony domestic battery – that causing serious injury.
71 Arizona, Connecticut, Washington D.C., Iowa, Hawaii, Maine, Missouri, Nevada, New Jersey, Oregon, Rhode Island, South Dakota, Utah, Washington, Wisconsin.
72 Blakely, C. (2007) 'Prisons, Penology and Penal Reform: An Introduction to Institutional Specialisation', New York: Peter Lang.
73 And any arrest, even if not followed by a charge, has to be declared when travelling to the United States, for example: https://uk.usembassy.gov/visas/visa-waiver-program/additional-requirements/.
74 In the Milwaukee Domestic Violence Project evaluation, for employed suspects, arrest reduced the frequency rate of repeat violence by 16%; for unemployed suspects, arrest increased the frequency of repeat violence by 44% – though this might be linked to

The same principle was articulated by the Judge when sentencing CG; no punitive conditions needed to be added to the SSO, on the basis that she had been punished, and, implicitly, deterred from any further offending, by her experience of a lengthy prosecution of a complex multi-handed conspiracy to defraud:[75]

> I do not think that that SSO needs any add-on provisions. This has been a salutary lesson to you in life and I don't think you need the National Probation Service to teach you any more lessons. I am certain this is the one and only time the criminal courts will see you.

Effectively, the sentiment here was that no punishment nor deterrence was needed, on the basis that the personal circumstances, and those of the offence, which the Judge had recited earlier in his sentencing comments, pointed to this being an offence by a middle-aged woman of previous good character in thrall to a manipulative and abusive partner whose criminal will she enacted for a shorter time than other defendants. It is interesting that the Judge does not differentiate between the notions of punishment and deterrence, and indeed appears to be regarding them as analogous as per the Classical model – the 'lesson in life' being both the punishment received, and the resultant deterrence preventing further offending (see Chapter 2).

A Judge can impose no punishment at all – through discharging the offender absolutely or conditionally, as explained in the Introduction. A good example of when a discharge will be appropriate is where the underlying cause of the offending is being addressed by some other means. DL was prosecuted by the local authority for failing to send her 15-year-old son, K, to school, and convicted after trial. In giving her reasons for convicting DL, the District Judge had said:[76]

> This is a very difficult situation. I have some very considerable sympathy with you. When 15-year-old boys grow and are as tall as adult men, but mentally and emotionally still little boys inside this large frame, they are difficult creatures to deal with. But you need as a parent to be firm and consistent and not resort to emotional blackmail. I believe your evidence about your own [health] problems but where you were not reasonable or justified is when you warn him that Social Services are going

neighbourhood censure resulting from the arrest – Sherman, L. W. (1992) Attacking Crime: Police and Crime Control, *Crime and Justice*, 15(1), pp. 159–230, at p. 206.

75 *R v CG*, Teesside Crown Court, 27th March 2018.

76 *London Borough of X v DL*, Highbury Corner Magistrates' Court, 23rd July 2018.

to become involved and he threatens, and teenage boys do, to leave, that is when the parent must put their foot down and say 'K, if you don't change your behaviour it will happen', and you have got to stand up to your son and not let him push you around. He is self-conscious, and obviously embarrassed about struggling and will not want to be teased by classmates as no one likes that. That is all the more reason to get the help that he needs. [...] You are the mother, you have the legal responsibility. The law means he has to be in school. The Education Welfare Officer is not busybody, she is there to protect the welfare of your son. She has a legal duty and responsibility to do what she has. I consider despite your obvious difficulties you didn't do all you could have – there is far more that you could have done. Don't let him bully you. I find there was a failure to attend school, no reasonable justification for K's absences and for those reasons I find you guilty of this offence.

By the adjourned sentencing hearing, DL had sought help from social services to manage her son's behaviour. Making it clear that it was purely on the basis of that voluntary engagement with social services, the Judge imposed an absolute discharge on DL.

A balancing act – punishment and other aims

As DL's case illustrates, balancing punishment with other aims which may better serve the utilitarian imperative of desistance from offending by addressing underlying issues is often a finely balanced exercise. An example comes from the sentencing of RA, for breaches of an SSO imposed for multiple thefts by an employee:[77]

Judge after Judge has been lenient with you. You've got plenty of experience. You were breached regarding the 2014 matter[78] and this is now the second time of failing to comply with the second order.[79] How you aren't in prison I don't know – you ought to be. Either I lock you up for 6 or 9 months as I was going to, or I seek some more positive way of dealing with it, at the same time punishing you for your completely hopeless response to chances offered. I must make it plain to you that court orders are not optional extras – they take precedence. I am pleased to hear that your wife's health has improved and you're in

---

77 *R v RA*, Central Criminal Court, 2nd May 2017.
78 In 2014 RA had received an SSO for non-dwelling burglary and theft.
79 Imposed for the theft by an employee offence.

work; it would cause disproportionate wreckage to others if I lock you up and you come out as bad as before.

It is interesting here that the Judge characterised the punishment as resulting from RA's 'completely hopeless response to chances offered' – that 'completely hopeless response' being failing to attend probation meetings as required by the SSO. Therefore, the Judge was punishing RA for breach of the SSO but characterised it by reference to the fact that by not being sent to custody for the offence, RA had been offered a chance. The frustration expressed by Judges when defendants breach SSOs and COs is a theme picked up again in Chapter 3, on rehabilitation.

Conclusion

Whilst punishment may seem the obvious place to start when considering sentencing, this chapter has identified a number of ways in which measuring and imposing punishment as part of a sentence for a criminal offence is not straightforward. Even imprisonment can be interpreted as punishment in different ways – either in and of itself, or through conditions during imprisonment. Many serious offenders have to be dealt with by the imposition of custody, at least in the short term, for protection of the public (see Chapter 4). Where an offender is teetering on the custody threshold, or facing a shorter term of imprisonment, many would argue that the starting position should be avoiding imprisonment. For example, in Norway, the entire prison population fluctuates between around 2,500 and 3,500 prisoners, and a rate of around 60 per 100,000 of the population.[80] Nonetheless, Norway has an extremely low recidivism rate: around 20%.[81] The Nordic embrace of penal exceptionalism, with prison *as* punishment instead of *for* punishment,[82] is in stark contrast to the English system.

Despite strong evidence that many offenders could benefit from purely rehabilitative sentencing disposals, the Government removed a clear way of delivering that by imposing a requirement that all COs must contain a punitive element. Chapter 3's exploration of rehabilitation illustrates why

---

80 www.prisonstudies.org/country/norway [accessed 25th November 2020] – but figures used are those from the graphs showing 2000–2018, as the up-to-date figures from April 2020 could be skewed by coronavirus.

81 Kristofferson, R. (2010) Relapse study in the correctional services of Nordic consequences www.kriminalomsorgen.no/getfile.php/4725234.823.usuksitb7p7qsm/Nordic%2Brel apse%2Bstudy%2Babstract%2B.pdf [accessed 25th November 2020].

82 Pakes, F and Gunlaugsson, H. (2018) A more Nordic Norway: Examining Prisons in 21st Century Iceland, *The Howard Journal*, 57(2), pp. 137–151.

this is a regrettable move in the context of a system that should be aiming to reduce recidivism by the most effective means, as opposed to focussing on politically motivated manoeuvres. Politically focussed changes tend to address matters concerning which better public legal education about sentencing options, and the reasons Judges impose the sentences they do, could lead to a greater understanding of why imprisonment is often not the option most likely to reduce re-offending.

2 Sentencing (to reduce crime, and) as deterrence

> Deterrence: Deterring or preventing by fear.
>
> (Oxford English Dictionary)

As early as 1889, Baker noted that the punishment to be preferred is that which combines the greatest deterrence with the least pain.[1] In this way, it can be extremely difficult to separate the contents of this chapter from the contents of Chapter 1 – indeed, one of the things that was noticeable in writing this book was how often Judges seem to conflate the notions of punishment and deterrence. It could be said that they are different sides of the same coin: in response to an offence, backward-looking punishment penalises that offence, whilst forward-looking deterrence seeks to prevent further offences. However, it has been suggested that deterrence can operate without actual punishment – that the thought or threat of punishment can be sufficient.[2] This is the basis for general deterrence, which operates on wider society, as opposed to specific deterrence, operating on those who are themselves punished.

This chapter sets out briefly the theoretical bases of deterrence, acknowledging that they are fundamentally intertwined with our notions of punishment. In recognition of this, it also explores whether, and if so, how, reduction in crime can be possible in circumstances without punishment within an adversarial criminal justice system – an exploration continued in the following chapter on rehabilitation.

The theory of deterrence as recognisable in England and Wales has developed from the philosophical works of Hobbes,[3] Beccaria,[4] and

---

1 Baker, T. B. L. (1889) 'War with Crime', p. 124.
2 Durlauf, S. N. and Nagin, D. S. (2011) Imprisonment and Crime: Can both be reduced?, *Criminology and Public Policy*, 10(1), pp. 13–54.
3 Hobbes, T. (1651) 'Leviathan'.
4 Beccaria, C. (1764) 'On Crimes and Punishments'.

DOI: 10.4324/9781003201625-2

Bentham.[5] Hobbes theorised the 'social contract'; the implicit agreement of all members of society to act in ways that do not always follow their own egocentric desires, providing all other citizens do the same, in recognition that if everyone followed their own desires and acted only in self-interest, the exclusion of parts of society would lead to crime and disorder. To enforce this social contract, it will be necessary that the state punish those who transgress it. Where this is necessary, the punishment for the crime must be greater than the benefit derived from committing it. This notion will be returned to later in this chapter. Hobbes did not go so far as to say to what extent the punishment could be greater than the benefit derived.

Beccaria, a Classical Italian thinker, built on the idea of the social contract to specify further the characteristics that punishment should take. He argued that if the only purpose of punishment is to prevent crime, 'punishments are unjust when their severity exceeds what is necessary to achieve deterrence'.[6] This, of course, requires a careful calibration of how great the severity required is to deter each individual – this thorny question of individualised sentences again rears its head as it did in Chapter 1.

At a similar time, Bentham was concluding the same in the UK. He viewed the role of the state as promoting the happiness of society, by punishing wrongdoing and rewarding those who acted in ways that supported and enriched society. He started from the position that a legislator's first aim must be to prevent offending,[7] but that where that cannot be achieved, the aim should be to divert an offender towards the least severe offence that will achieve his aims,[8] and punish at the lowest level possible.[9] Punishment in excess of that essential to deter law-breaking is therefore unjustified in Bentham's perception, as it was for Beccaria.

Deterrence or desistance?

Much academic literature focuses on what happens within an offender's self-identification when they cease committing offences. Most notably, there is a widely accepted distinction between primary and secondary desistance.[10]

---

5 Bentham, J. (1781) 'An Introduction to the Principles of Morals and Legislation'.

6 See above, fn 4.

7 Bentham, J. (1781) 'An Introduction to the Principles of Morals and Legislation', Chapter XIV, II, and III.1.

8 *Ibid*, at IV.2 and V.3.

9 *Ibid*, at VI.4.

10 Maruna, S. and Farrall, S. (2004) Desistance from crime: A theoretical reformulation, *Kolner Zeitschrift fur Soziologie und Sozialpsychologie*, 43, pp. 171–194.

Primary desistance describes a temporary cessation of offending – something many long-term offenders have done at times during their lives, before then committing further offences. Secondary desistance, meanwhile, is the transformation of self-identity from that of an offender to that of a non-offender – a cessation of criminal behaviour forming part of who they are. Many sentences are aimed at primary desistance, or in the case of particularly prolific offenders, the reduction in the frequency and/or severity of their offending. There are clear arguments in favour of a sentencing option that focusses on the attainment of secondary desistance. However, throughout this book it is clear that the current system in England would struggle to provide such an option, considering already the real difficulties in finding resources to provide rehabilitative programmes in prison (see Chapter 4) and cuts to the Probation Service, meaning that news stories questioning whether offenders who committed offences whilst on probation were being properly supervised[11] are not as rare as would be hoped.[12]

Privatisation of parts of the National Probation Service's role through using Community Rehabilitation Companies (CRCs) was again aimed at providing a more diverse range of programmes with which those on Community Orders or Suspended Sentence Orders could engage. It was by no means a clear success. Some CRCs received scathing criticism for their inadequacies in keeping the public safe; for example, an inspection in 2020[13] of the Hampshire and Isle of Wight CRC reported that the service was 'inadequate' in the areas of assessment, planning, implementation and delivery, and reviewing under the umbrella of case supervision.[14]

11 For example Usman Khan, who committed two terrorist murders whilst being supervised by the National Probation Service – early indications suggest that those who were responsible for his supervision did not have sufficient, if any, experience of supervising offenders who had been convicted of terrorist offences www.bbc.co.uk/news/uk-england-london-545 73750 [accessed 4th November 2020]. An independent report by Jonathan Hall QC was commissioned, and published in May 2020 https://assets.publishing.service.gov.uk/gove rnment/uploads/system/uploads/attachment_data/file/913983/supervision-terrorism-and-t errorism-risk-offenders-review.pdf [accessed 4th November 2020].

12 Where these offences are classed as serious, they trigger a 'Serious Further Offence' review. This review process itself was the subject of Her Majesty's Inspectorate of Probation (2020) A thematic inspection of the Serious Further Offences (SFO) investigation and review process, London: HMIP. It is important to remember that as a proportion of the whole number of those who are being supervised at any time by the NPS and CRCs, those who commit serious offences form a tiny minority – though sometimes a high profile one.

13 That was cut short by the coronavirus pandemic, meaning no overall score could be given, but discrete areas were still able to be assessed.

14 HMI Probation (2020) An inspection of probation services in: Hampshire and Isle of Wight Community Rehabilitation Company, London: Her Majesty's Inspectorate of Probation, at

It was noted that this decline from the previous rating in January 2019 of 'Good' in those areas resulted directly from cuts to funding which inhibited the CRC's ability to recruit experienced practitioners:[15]

> It was the only CRC to achieve this rating ['Good'] in our year one inspection programme. It is therefore disappointing to find a sharp decline in the quality of case supervision since the previous inspection. We have concluded that this directly relates to a shortfall in sufficiently trained and experienced practitioners in this service.

When assessing the seven divisions of the National Probation Service (NPS) which retained responsibility for supervising those offenders judged to be the highest risk to the public, a report by the inspectorate found that:[16]

> Over the past year, Her Majesty's Inspectorate of Probation has inspected all seven NPS divisions against 10 different quality standards and given each of them an overall rating. While none of the divisions were rated 'Outstanding', five out of seven were rated 'Good' and none were found to be 'Inadequate'. In general, the quality of case supervision delivered by NPS staff was found to better than that delivered by their CRC equivalents – particularly in relation to the management of risk of harm to the public.

These short excerpts illustrate some of the difficulties being faced in recruiting and retaining staff who have sufficient knowledge and professional experience to supervise challenging offenders, and also the need for sufficient resources to enable them to do so thoroughly. Whilst this part of the system remains underfunded it is hard to argue that community sentences can fulfil their potential in effecting deterrence through a combination of punishment, rehabilitation, and general support.

The requirement, introduced through the Crime and Courts Act 2013, that Community Orders contain at least one element for punishment suggests that the legislature has accepted as a theoretical concept that it is not possible to deter without the imposition of punishment. This is a disappointing

---

p. 6 justiceinspectorates.gov.uk/hmiprobation/wp-content/uploads/sites/5/2020/07/HIOW -CRC-1.pdf [accessed 4th November 2020].

15 *Ibid*, at p. 4.

16 Her Majesty's Inspectorate of Probation (2020) An inspection of central functions supporting the National Probation Service, London: HMIP, at p. 4, www.justiceinspectorates.gov .uk/hmiprobation/wp-content/uploads/sites/5/2020/01/NPS-central-functions-inspection -report-1.pdf [accessed 4th November 2020].

conclusion which, as explored in Chapter 3, does not seem to be under-pinned by research.

Due to the popular perception that deterrence is effected most efficiently through punishment, and limitations such as those within the supervision of community-based sentences, the courts often have to use blunter tools to try to effect deterrence. This might be the sentence itself – which can be aimed at deterring the individual from further offences, or the general public, on hearing about the case.[17] Alternatively, it might be through matters ancillary to the sentence that deterrence is attempted, such as a mandatory driving disqualification, which may in fact cause the offender greater inconvenience or hardship than a fine. This was articulated by the Circuit Judge, sitting with two lay magistrates, who rejected JB's appeal against sentence, in which it was submitted that she should not be subject to the mandatory disqualification that results under s.35 Road Traffic Offenders Act (RTOA) 1988 from amassing 12 or more penalty points:[18]

> We entirely accept that you have been placed in a position of hardship and inconvenience as result of disqualification. However the law is strict and we need to find exceptional circumstances. The inconvenience is to you and your care for your parents and we commend that. However, that is not in itself dependent on you having a driving licence. The way the law deals with those who speed, including the totting provisions, is severe but that is for a reason – those of us who work in these courts see the consequences of speeding. [...] the penalty will not be interfered with.

17 Some may suggest that this proposition falls down due to the generally poor level of accuracy in the reporting of cases and sentencing disposals. For example, a paper reported that someone had been convicted of burglary of a property, when in fact he had been convicted only of handling stolen goods that had been taken from the property – after a report was made to the Independent Press Standards Organisation (IPSO), and an investigation had begun (Resolution Statement 01321-20 *A man v Sunday Life*), the publication concerned agreed to publish a correction: www.ipso.co.uk/rulings-and-resoluti on-statements/ruling/?id=01321-20 [accessed 17th November 2020]. In another case IPSO investigated (Resolution Statement 12281-20 *A woman v The Mail* (Cumbria)), the journalist had wrongly reported that the defendant had had a warrant issued for her arrest on non-attendance when she had been excused, and confused the drink drive limit in England with that in Scotland, with the consequence that he had reported that the woman was over the drink drive limit by a far greater proportion than was in fact the case – mediation resolved the complaint as a clarification was published www.ipso.c o.uk/rulings-and-resolution-statements/ruling/?id=12281-20 [accessed 17th November 2020].

18 *R v JB*, Woolwich Crown Court, 20th May 2016.

The same thought process was echoed on the other side of London, when a Circuit Judge and two magistrates in St Albans heard an appeal against the disqualification imposed on 'totters' on the basis of similar arguments, and were similarly unpersuaded, refusing an appeal against a sentence imposed by the magistrates' court on MH in the following terms:[19]

> MH has been disqualified as a totter.[20] MH appeals against the disqualification element of the penalty imposed in the court below on the basis of exceptional hardship. Section 35 of the Road Traffic Offenders Act is relevant. Subsection 1 provides that when D reaches 12 or more penalty points the court must order disqualification for not less than 6 months, unless having regard to all circumstances there are grounds for mitigating the normal consequences. [...] We have heard evidence from him regarding the impact on several elements of his life. His company, his health, his family and his voluntary work. For all of those reasons there is no doubt that disqualification would have an adverse effect on his personal and professional lives. That is the point of the penalty. Loss of one's driving licence in the modern world causes real difficulties. For that reason it is a substantial deterrent. We have given particularly careful consideration to the impact on his children, parents and staff. We are not persuaded that he has taken all possible steps to investigate alternatives. We are not persuaded that the hardship is genuinely exceptional. The appeal is refused and penalties remain.

The notion that a punishment imposed on one individual can deter others is one that is central to our criminal justice system, as illustrated through a number of the sentencing remarks set out in the next section. However, this relies on high quality, accurate court reporting, something many newspapers no longer prioritise, with court correspondents often attending only snippets of cases and thus not being able to report fully the aspects of the case that led to the imposition of a particular sentence, allowing the public to understand the relationship between the offence and the sentence received. The importance of the details of a case to whether the public view the sentence as appropriate is well-established.[21]

---

19 *R v MH*, St Albans Crown Court, 10th May 2018.
20 This is a colloquial term for someone who has amassed 12 penalty points on their licence through separate offences (e.g. sets of 3 points for fairly moderate speeding offences), meaning that when all their points are 'totted up' they fall to be disqualified under section 35 of the Road Traffic Offenders Act 1988.
21 E.g. Roberts, J., Hough, M., Jacobson, J., and Moon, N. (2009) Public Attitudes to Sentencing Purposes and Sentencing Factors: An Empirical Analysis, *Criminal Law Review*, pp. 771–782.

In *R v Felixstowe Justices, ex parte Leigh*,[22] it was held that:

> in exercising the inherent power of a court to control the conduct of its proceedings, justices should neither discourage fair and accurate reporting of the proceedings nor depart from the general rule of open justice to any extent greater than the court reasonably believed necessary in order to serve the ends of justice; that open justice required that no member of a court could seek anonymity and the names of justices must not be withheld from the parties, their legal representatives, the press in court reporting the proceedings and a bona fide inquirer.

Watkins LJ, giving the leading judgment with which Mann J and Russell J agreed, observed:[23]

> The role of the journalist and his importance for the public interest in the administration of justice has been commented upon on many occasions. No one nowadays surely can doubt that his presence in court for the purpose of reporting proceedings conducted therein is indispensable. Without him, how is the public to be informed of how justice is being administered in our courts?

This echoed (and indeed Watkins LJ referred to) an earlier passage written by Lord Denning in his 1955 book *The Road To Justice*, in which he wrote that:[24]

> A newspaper reporter is in every court. He sits through the dullest cases in the Court of Appeal and the most trivial cases before the magistrates. He says nothing but writes a lot; he is, I verily believe, the watchdog of justice.

However, Lord Denning's reasoning for conferring this title on journalists was not that the communication to the public at large led to deterrence for those who might be considering the same crime, but instead because public scrutiny encouraged those who worked in the courts to behave properly:[25]

> The reason for this rule is the very salutary influence which publicity has for those who work in the light of it. The judge will be careful to

---

22 [1987] QB 582 – at this time the quality and depth of legal reporting across all media was arguably much higher than in the present day.

23 *Ibid*, at p. 591.

24 Denning, A. (1955) *The Road to Justice*, London: Stevens and Sons, at p. 64.

25 *Ibid.*

see that the trial is fairly and properly conducted if he realises that any unfairness or impropriety on his part will be noted by those in court and may be reported in the press. He will be more anxious to give a correct decision if he knows that his reasons must justify themselves at the bar of public opinion.

General and specific deterrence

It may be tempting to put aside concerns at the efficacy of accurately communicating court proceedings, including sentencing outcomes, to the public through the press. However, one of the reasons why everyday sentencing exercises form a worthwhile basis for this book, as an under-appreciated aspect of the criminal justice system, is that the reporting of such cases in any depth and accuracy is very rare. Nonetheless, it is upon this public knowledge that the theory of general deterrence rests. General deterrence posits that it is possible that the prosecution and sentencing of one person could cause others to refrain from the same behaviour: deterrence has both a personal and a societal dimension. Specific deterrence – that aimed at the individual who has committed this crime to dissuade them from committing further crimes, has a much narrower focus than general deterrence. General deterrence uses the experience of a specific individual, communicated to society, to dissuade others from committing the offence that the specific individual committed. As noted by Blakely,[26] this is an important distinction: in specific deterrence, a crime has already been committed by the person it is hoped will be deterred in the future. General deterrence hopes to deter those who have not yet committed any crime by the illustration of the experiences of the person who has.

When sentencing MA,[27] the Judge explained why the sentence had to be immediate custody for perverting the course of justice where MA had attempted to collect a car from the police station. MA did this on the pretence that the car was his, likely to try to provide his friend B with a defence to the drug-dealing charge that had resulted from three men, including B, being seen by the car, acting suspiciously. B had the car keys in his possession, and a search of the car revealed five different varieties of drugs.

I have read the PSR (pre-sentence report) – it is not lengthy. Its suggestion is a non-custodial sentence but it is absolutely essential that people

---

26 Blakely, C. (2007) 'Prisons, Penology and Penal Reform: An Introduction to Institutional Specialisation', New York: Peter Lang, at p. 20.
27 *R v MA*, Isleworth Crown Court, 7th March 2018.

realise that if they are going to tell lies with the intention to pervert the course of justice lengthy sentences, and sentences of immediate imprisonment, will follow. The least sentence that I can pass in this case, taking into account [the guilty plea] discount, is 15 months' imprisonment.

A decision to prioritise a deterrent message for society, however, can often mean that other aspects of s.57 have to be subordinated. When sentencing YH for possession of articles for use in fraud,[28] the Judge said,

The main offence is so serious that only custody may follow. In my judgment the need for deterrence in such cases means rehabilitation prospects are outweighed. Others need to know that offences like this will be penalised to protect the integrity of the financial systems.

The extent to which sending a deterrent message to society may mean a harsher outcome for the specific defendant is entirely dependent upon the sentencing Judge. In that way, despite the Sentencing Guidelines, sentences can be tempered to the circumstances of the defendant. Often this is reflected in a decision to suspend imprisonment. This was expressed in JZ,[29] when the Judge was sentencing for an immigration offence involving the smuggling of a baby, which case law indicates will usually lead to immediate imprisonment;

In all those circumstances, despite deterrence, I don't think that means that everyone who comes to this court having committed this offence must automatically receive a deterrent sentence. This is an unusual case and I treat you as an exception if only as the result of what you have been through.

Similarly the sentencing bench of magistrates dealing with DeL's case[30] took notice of her own health, and the fact that she was caring for her husband, whose health was even poorer. They decided that the appropriate way to deter DeL from the specific sort of offence that she had committed (driving whilst disqualified) was a further period of disqualification, but a less harsh 'main' sentence – a fine instead of a Community Order:

We have listened carefully to your advocate and we've taken a lot of what she has said on board. But we are concerned that you still have a

---

28 *R v YH*, Harrow Crown Court, 17th April 2019.
29 *R v JZ*, Isleworth Crown Court, 27th July 2017.
30 *R v DeL* (to differentiate from DL in Chapter 1), Uxbridge Magistrates' Court, 30th June 2016.

car at your disposal. This was a foolish thing to do and we feel we must mark it and give you another deterrent as if you do it again leniency may not be an option. So we are going to disqualify you from today for 12 months. We are told by the guidelines to add at least another 6 but we have shown you that leniency, as the effective extension on your current disqualification will be 4 months. We should have looked at a high-level Community Order but you clearly have enough on your plate and you're not a well woman. We are going to fine you – we looked carefully at your means form and we are not going to give you a Band D, as the PSR encourages, we're going to give a Band C fine and at the lower end – £160.

Nonetheless, the idea of deterrence surfaces regularly when criminal justice matters are being discussed in Parliament, such as the following example from the debate about amendments to legislation to introduce a mandatory minimum term of imprisonment for any adult found carrying a knife in public:[31]

The House should require courts to send a clear and unequivocal message about carrying a knife. If we need more convincing that the message that people should not carry knives is currently weak, we need look no further than the thousands of children who do not regard it as a serious offence.

That legislation was passed, and is now enshrined within s.315 of the Sentencing Act 2020. It imposes a mandatory minimum sentence of six months' imprisonment for any adult (18 or over) who is convicted of having an offensive weapon in a public place (s.1(1) Prevention of Crime Act 1953), or an article with a blade or a point in a public place (s.139(1) Criminal Justice Act 1998) when that person has previously been convicted of the same offence. Where someone aged 16 or 17 is convicted of such an offence, the mandatory minimum is a four-month Detention and Training Order (DTO).[32]

When sentencing II,[33] who had a previous conviction for carrying a knife, the Judge was clear that the mandatory minimum was for both general and specific deterrence and was thus justified for II. II was being sentenced for two separate offences committed to the Crown Court for sentence by the magistrates' court. The first was possession of an offensive weapon (a

---

31 Hansard, 17th June 2014, Column 1012–1013.
32 The mandatory sentence does not apply where the offender is under 16.
33 II, Inner London Crown Court, 26th July 2016.

'rambo' knife) in a public place in March 2016, and the second was having an article with a blade or a point (a carving knife with a nine-inch blade) in June 2016. He was just 18, and had been convicted for the first time earlier in 2016 for possession of heroin and cocaine, and having an article with a blade or a point. Sentencing him, the Judge said:

> You have pleaded guilty to a number of serious offences relating to knives. In relation to the June matter the facts placed before me on your behalf are you were simply in the car [as opposed to having the knife on his person] and this makes no significant difference to sentence as far as I can see – I sentence you on the basis that you remained in the car at all times. An aggravating feature in all of this is the accumulating number of these sorts of offences. This is your second offence whilst under an SSO for a lock knife imposed in April. The 30th of June matter is in breach of that SSO. The 18th of March matter is not.
>
> I am told on your behalf that this behaviour with knives began following an attack on you in December last year when you were severely knifed and wounded yourself and ended up in the intensive care unit; as a result of that you started to carry knives. I'm told you are an intelligent person and understand this already: This is an important fact for you and for all of the community in London: Carrying a knife is extremely dangerous for you and everyone else in society. That's why Parliament have instituted a minimum of 6 months' imprisonment for carrying knives. In this case notwithstanding that you have done well at school and are looking for a job, you've decided to go down the route of arming yourself with a knife in response to the attack on you. That was the wrong response. You must understand how serious this is.
>
> I take into account your age, and that before the attack in December you were leading a law-abiding life. But I must impose custody on you due to the number of these offences. [...] You must understand that this must stop. You must not carry a knife when you are released.

II received four months' detention for the March offence; six months detention for the June offence, and the Judge activated the entirety of the 12-week suspended sentence, though he made the three sentences concurrent to further reflect mitigation. Unfortunately, deterrence did not work for this young man. In June 2019, II was convicted of attempted murder after shooting a man outside a takeaway in Brixton.[34] He was sentenced to

---

34 This case was reported in the mainstream media, but a reference is not provided as that would reveal the identity of the client.

21 years' imprisonment for that offence, with other concurrent sentences being imposed for three other separate offences.

Deterrence and mandatory minima

A second offence of possessing an offensive weapon is one example of the small number of offences where the sentencing Judge has even less discretion in the sentence that they impose: these are offences that carry a minimum sentence of imprisonment for repeat offenders who have committed an offence of that type previously.

Arguably such minimum sentences are hoped to have both a specific and a general deterrent effect. Possession of a knife is not the only offence carrying such a mandatory minimum. The most well-known mandatory minimum in England is the life sentence for murder, which has existed since 1965, when capital punishment was abolished (Murder (Abolition of Death Penalty) Act 1965). Variations in culpability for the murder are then reflected through the setting of the tariff period – that being the amount of time that the offender will be required to spend in custody before they can apply to the Parole Board to be released on licence.[35] Since November 2002, and the House of Lords decision in *Anderson v Secretary of State*[36] this tariff has been set by the trial Judge, guided by Schedule 21 to the Criminal Justice Act 2003. Schedule 21 sets out different starting points depending on the facts of the offence. This includes a 'whole life order' – the only sentence in England that requires the offender to be detained by the state for the rest of their natural life.[37]

In addition to the mandatory minimum for a second offence of possession of an offensive weapon or a bladed article, mandatory minima for repeat offenders also exist for a third domestic burglary (three years)[38] and a third trafficking of Class A drugs offence (seven years).[39]

Two further mandatory minima apply the first time an offender commits the relevant offence; possessing firearms that are prohibited weapons,[40] and threatening with a weapon or bladed article.[41] All of the mandatory minima

---

35 S.269 Criminal Justice Act 2003.
36 [2003] 1 AC 837.
37 Although this is the only sort of sentence that mandates life-long imprisonment, other types of sentence can lead to the same situation – most notably the now-abolished Imprisonment for Public Protection, or 'IPP' sentence, which is discussed in full in Chapter 4.
38 S.314 SA 20.
39 S.313 SA 20.
40 S.311 SA 20 and Schedule 20.
41 S.312 SA 20.

contain clauses allowing disapplication if there are exceptional circumstances relating to the offence or the offender which justify not imposing
the mandatory minimum.

It is noteworthy that three of the mandatory minima provisions apply
only on a second or third offence – i.e. where the first sentence did evi-
dently not deter the offender from committing the same offence again.
Alternative analyses would be that the first sentence did not rehabilitate
the offender from their criminal tendencies; or that because the offender
was not deterred or rehabilitated, the criminal justice system now needs
to protect the public from the offender committing further offences, and
the rationale is simply one of a perceived necessity for incapacitation.
This does not, however, give a sound theoretical underpinning for which
offences have mandatory minima, and neither is there any clarity as to
why mandatory minima may be more likely to deter in relation to those
offences than others.

A mandatory minimum sentence will, of course, reduce crime in the
community in the short term, as the offender will necessarily be imprisoned
unless they have been able to convince the sentencing court that they fall
within a circumstance which would make the mandatory minimum unjust,
or justify it not being applied. Whether it will have a longer-term effect
will be likely to depend upon the rehabilitation that is available to those
offenders whilst they are imprisoned – a topic returned to in Chapter 3. It
is impossible to quantify the deterrent aspect, as that could only be discov-
ered through an in-depth study of the likelihood of re-offending by those
who have received mandatory minimum sentences compared with those
who have not. However, taking a wider view of what is known about the
criminogenic consequences of imprisonment, it seems unlikely that simply
imprisoning offenders for longer on the basis of a mandatory minimum will
in fact deter them from committing further offences.[42]

Enhanced sentencing for certain offences motivated by actual or perceived personal characteristics

An alternative approach to mandatory minima is to impose an 'uplift' when
sentencing for a specific group of offences. This is present in English law

---

42 Some American-based research has suggested that the imposition of the death penalty
reduces the rate of single-offence murder convictions. However, it did not have the same
effect on multiple-murder convictions – Ekelund Jr., R. B., Jackson, J. D., Ressler, R. W.,
and Tollison, R. D. (2006) Marginal Deterrence and Multiple Murder, *Southern Economic
Journal*, 72(3), p. 521.

in relation to hate crimes – offences committed against someone because of that person's actual or perceived attributes of race, religion, sexuality, disability, or transgender status.[43]

Section 66 of the SA 20[44] applies when a court is considering any offence other than one of those that is intrinsically a hate crime – i.e. where one of the elements that the prosecution has to prove is that the offence was motivated by (or the offender demonstrated) hostility towards a personal characteristic of the victim. Therefore, where a court is sentencing for any other offence 'which is aggravated by racial hostility, religious hostility, hostility related to disability, hostility related to sexual orientation, or hostility related to transgender identity',[45] it must treat that fact as an aggravating factor,[46] and must state in open court that the offence was so aggravated.[47]

It is important to note, however, that enhanced sentencing does not allow a court to sentence above the maximum that is available for the offence. This is an important limitation, as where a summary-only offence is aggravated by hostility to a group recognised in s.66, the six-month maximum for a single offence that the magistrates' court can impose remains, meaning that if the offence was already a very bad example of its kind, there may be little additional penalty that can be added.[48] This means that the symbolic recognition of the 'hostility' element of the offence is watered down.

It also leads to questions about the theoretical justification for enhanced sentences for hate crimes against certain groups. Is it to deter those who have discriminatory thoughts from committing criminal offences motivated by them? If they assault someone as a result of their prejudice against that person's characteristics, but disguise its true motivation, then they will get a lesser sentence. Is it to inflict greater punishment justified on the basis of the societally unacceptable views motivating the offence? Cavadino observes

---

43 At the time of writing, the Law Commission has just published a Consultation Paper ('CP') on Hate Crime – Law Commission (2020) Hate Crime Laws: A Consultation Paper, Consultation Paper 250, London: HMSO. The huge body of academic literature examining the potential justifications for the current criminal law response to hate crime, and the criminalisation of, and/or enhanced sentencing for, hostility towards additional characteristics, is summarised throughout the CP.

44 Previously s.145 CJA 03.

45 S.66(1)(a)–(e) SA 20.

46 S.66(2)(a) SA 20.

47 S.66(2)(b) SA 20.

48 There are no Sentencing Council guidelines on what amount the uplift should be – whether it is an absolute figure or a proportion of the non-uplifted sentence, and what absolute figure or proportion it ought to be.

that the assumption that harsher sentencing for hate crimes is justified can and should be interrogated for its rationale.[49] He notes that such sentences are unlikely to reduce the occurrence of hate crime or to increase the satisfaction of victims. However, a moderate increase in sentence may be justifiable to reflect that hate crimes may typically cause more harm than non-hate-motivated offences, thus requiring greater punishment for the offender.

It is largely agreed amongst academics that hate crime can be said to cause greater harm to both the direct victim, and others who share their targeted characteristic,[50] than non-hate-motivated offences,[51] and reflect greater culpability on the part of the offenders.[52] However, the only theoretical justification for enhanced sentencing is that it is symbolic – by punishing additionally for the hate, it is demarcating the hate itself as an additional wrong to the offence itself – an argument that did not convince the Law Commission in their 2020 Consultation on Hate Crime.[53]

Perhaps more appealing than simply imposing longer sentences for crimes with certain attributes – a practice that relies entirely on 'pure' deterrence of the harsher punishment directly correlating with more offenders taking a decision not to commit that sort of crime – is the 'Sword of Damocles', an apocryphal item written about by Cicero. This theory presupposes 'ever-present peril' – in criminological circumstances, that if someone knows that if they do something prohibited, their punishment will be definite and immediate, they are less likely to do it. When linked to writings that argue that it is the certainty of punishment, as opposed to its severity, that deters offenders,[54] a method that allows the threat of punishment to hang over offenders in a more concrete way could be said to represent a useful sentencing method.

---

49 Cavadino, M. (2014) Should Hate Crime Be Sentenced More Severely?, *Contemporary Issues in Law*, 13(1), p. 5.

50 Walters, M. A., Paterson, J., McDonnell, L., and Brown, R. (2019) Group Identity, empathy and shared suffering: Understanding the Community impact of anti-LGBT and Islamophobic hate crime, *International Review of Victimology* 1, p. 17.

51 E.g. Chalmers, J. and Leverick, F. (2017) A Comparative Analysis of Hate Crime Legislation (University of Glasgow, 2017) para 3.1.1. p. 25. https://consult.gov.scot/hate-crime/independent-review-of-hate-crimelegislation/supporting_documents/495517_AP PENDIX%20%20ACADEMIC%20REPORT.pdf [accessed 18th November 2020].

52 E.g. Brax, D. (2016) 'Hate crime concepts and their moral foundations: a universal framework?', in J. Schweppe and M. A. Walters (eds), The Globalization of Hate: Internationalising Hate Crime?, Oxford: Oxford University Press, p. 61. Though this argument is robustly rejected by Hurd: Hurd, H. (2001) Why Liberals Should Hate 'Hate Crime Legislation', *Law and Philosophy*, 20, p. 215, 217.

53 Law Commission CP 250, at p. 55, para 17.40.

54 E.g. Durlauf, S. N. and Nagin, D. S. (2011) Imprisonment and Crime: Can both be reduced?, *Criminology and Public Policy*, 10(1), pp. 13–54.

Using the Sword of Damocles against corporate defendants

One illustration of the use of deterrence in the English criminal justice system is deferred prosecution agreements ('DPAs').[55] These are only available against companies,[56] and can only be applied for by the Serious Fraud Office ('SFO') and the Crown Prosecution Service. A small number have been secured since they were introduced in 2014,[57] all by the SFO. For a DPA to be entered into, the prosecution must have sufficient evidence to prosecute the company for an offence ('the evidential test') and it must be in the public interest to secure a DPA. However, if the company co-operates with the criminal investigation, and accepts a DPA, the criminal proceedings against the company are suspended.[58] Under a DPA the company must sort out its financial affairs, and tackle any offending behaviour of those within it, on pain of prosecution if it does not do so. This is a clear example of the 'Sword of Damocles' – if the company does not rectify the problems, it will face prosecution. So far, none of the nine DPAs approved by the court since 2015 have been breached, so no prosecution of a corporate body has followed. Therefore, there is not necessarily any immediate punishment (though a fine can be incorporated within the DPA, under Schedule 17, para 5(3)(a), in which case a punitive element is included – this has occurred in all of the DPAs in England so far, in addition to disgorgement of profits and costs), but instead the threat of future prosecution, and thus potential punishment, if the mismanagement that led to the offences charged is not rectified.

The Sword of Damocles and human defendants

The nearest alternative for an individual defendant, however, is a Judge deferring sentence.[59] This is crucially different to a DPA because it requires an individual to have been convicted of the offence, as opposed to there simply being enough evidence for a prosecution to commence. The Judge can then defer sentence for up to six months, but no longer, and can specify

---

55 Introduced by s.45 Crime and Courts Act 2013, with full provisions in Schedule 17 to that Act.
56 Though they are based on an American model, which is available against individuals as well.
57 Under s.1 of the Powers of Criminal Courts (Sentencing) Act 2000. The power had previously existed under s.22 Criminal Justice Act 1972, before being repealed by Powers of Criminal Courts Act 1973 (c. 62), Sch. 6.
58 Though individuals associated with it whose personal conduct meets the evidential test and the public interest test of the CPS Full Code Test can be charged and prosecuted separately in their own right.
59 Section 1 PCC(S)A 2000.

steps that must be taken within the period of the deferral. Those steps can be any that the court deems appropriate, and there is a specific power to defer for restorative justice activities to be undertaken[60] (see Chapter 5). The purpose of the deferral is to allow the court to assess the defendant's conduct after conviction, any change in their circumstances, and the extent of their compliance with the requirement imposed by the Judge. According to a Freedom of Information request made by the author,[61] 872 deferred sentences were imposed by Judges in Crown Courts in England and Wales in the calendar year 2019.[62]

In a recent case at St Albans Crown Court,[63] a Judge deferred sentence on DC as follows:

> In April 2018 you were seen driving a moped in appallingly dangerous circumstances which I have just viewed on CCTV. That sort of riding would be appalling enough from someone without an SSO hanging over them due to an SSO for causing serious injury by dangerous driving. If this case been brought to court in an appropriate timescale nothing would have saved you from going inside as you demonstrated contempt for the SSO by behaving in that way. It is now 2 years down line. You have not been in trouble since and I do not want, if I can possibly avoid it, to send a young man in his mid-20s to prison for the first time when there is a realistic prospect that you have learned your lesson and are not going to get into any more trouble in future. To give you an extended period of time to prove that to me, I am taking the unusual step of deferring sentence. You are subject to the deferred sentence order until 31st July. It doesn't require you to do anything, but sets two objectives:
>
> First is no criminal offences, so you had better stay out of trouble. Even if you have committed a very minor offence, including simple possession of cannabis, you will go straight inside on the next occasion.
>
> Second objective is sustained, repeated, genuine efforts to obtain work that are evidenced. Letters and emails from you and any supporting documents demonstrating what you have done to try to find work.

---

60 S.7 SA 20.
61 Freedom of Information request 200624014 to the Ministry of Justice, asking for the data on how many deferred sentences had been handed down in the Crown Court in the calendar year 2019.
62 The reason for using the calendar year 2019 is that the figures for 2020 could have been skewed by the coronavirus pandemic, which saw many Judges seek ways to keep 'borderline' cases out of prison in light of the judgment of the Court of Appeal (Criminal Division) in *Manning* [2020] EWCA Crim 592.
63 *R v DC*, St Albans Crown Court, 27th February 2020.

You are extraordinarily lucky – it is not your fault it took 18 months to get to the Magistrates' Court. You richly deserved custody, but you should have already served and been released from that.

It is noteworthy that one of the reasons for the deferral was that there had been a long delay between the offence and proceedings being instituted, and within this time the defendant had committed no further offences. Therefore, by requiring that status quo to remain until the end of July (five months later), the Judge had provided a strong deterrence from further offending. Any further offending, and the defendant knew that his sentence would be immediate custody. If he committed no further offences, then the likely outcome was that any period of custody imposed on the later date would be suspended.

When that defendant came back before the court in August,[64] he had abided by the terms of the deferral. The Judge specified the effect of the Sword of Damocles as a good reason why, for someone who was now showing themselves capable of being law-abiding, a Suspended Sentence Order, even of only a short custodial sentence, could be a way of dealing with an offender that was advantageous both to the offender and to society:

> Short sentences, even hanging over someone's head, are often not a good idea. Judges are reminded that very little can be achieved in a custodial setting when they are there for only a short time. Someone like you, I hope that with the threat of custody hanging over your head, will remind you, if you need it, to stay on the straight and narrow. The shortest sentence I can pass is 4 months imprisonment suspended for 18 months, considering your guilty plea. No further order for things that you must do during the course of that order – no unpaid work, curfew etc due to your other obligations. Commit any further offences and that will almost certainly be activated. You have demonstrated over 2 years that you can keep out of trouble.

It is an interesting contrast between the treatment of companies and individuals. A company could secure a DPA in an attempt to ward off a conviction. However for an individual, that approach is not available as an alternative to charge. Instead it is only available, to certain offenders, where charges have already proceeded, guilt has been established, and the incentive for the defendant is a lower sentence than they might otherwise have received (and often the difference between immediate and suspended custody).

---

64 The hearing was delayed to later within the six-month period permitted due to the coronavirus pandemic.

An individual-level agreement akin to a DPA would be an advanta-geous addition to the 'out of court disposals' such as conditional cautions. The charges could be suspended on the entering into a DPA-style agree-ment, with the full knowledge that if there were any further offences, or any further offences of a specified nature, a prosecution could be brought on the original facts. This would allow an offender, particularly a first time or very lightly convicted offender, to benefit from a second chance, whilst having the possibility of punishment acting as a deterrent against further criminality.

The reality, however, would be sadly wholly unachievable. For such a suggestion to work, there would need to be careful tailoring of the condi-tions of the deferral, if they were to be any more complex than not com-mitting any further crimes, or any further crimes of a specified sort, widely drawn (i.e. crimes relating to drugs, dishonesty offences, or violence). Further, there would need to be careful monitoring of the individual, a real-ity that for an already over-stretched Probation Service would not be a real-istic hope.

Another, slightly different, way in which the 'Sword of Damocles' can be hung over a defendant is by the use of an SSO. With a deferred sen-tence, 'the Sword' hangs over the offender for a period of up to six months between the deferral and the sentence being passed, with the incentive for law-abiding behaviour being the prospect of the lighter sentence at the end of deferral when sentencing. The conditions imposed can also be ones not available as part of a sentence[65] – for example to make evidenced efforts to find employment. With an SSO, 'the Sword' hangs over the offender for the length of the operational period, which can be between six months and two years, but the requirements that can be attached are more limited and criminal-justice specific, such as unpaid work or a curfew, plus thera-peutic requirements – those found in s.287 SA 20. The incentive for law-abiding behaviour – the commission of no further offences and abiding by any requirements, is the avoidance of the activation of (all or part of) the custodial term that has been suspended.

In this way, an SSO can sustain the Sword of Damocles for longer – up to two years as opposed to the six months under a deferred sentence. However, in contrast to a deferred sentence, the defendant does not have the possibility of a sentence lower than they would get if they did not com-ply. Nonetheless an SSO can be especially useful for first-time young adult offenders whose personal situation is generally stable, but whose offence

---

65 A deferred sentence being exactly that – a sentence that has not yet been passed, as it is deferred to a later date.

is sufficiently serious that the custody threshold[66] has been passed, and the sentencer wants to emphasise the seriousness of this offence whilst not wholly derailing a young person's life. This was evident in the case of CF, who had pleaded guilty to one offence of possession with intent to supply of Class A drugs:[67]

> You know, and accept, that this is a serious offence; the quantity is large and taking into account your culpability and the seriousness of this case I am satisfied this is category 4 and the starting point is immediate imprisonment of 18 months. The sentencing range is up to 3 years in prison for this offence. Having said that I take into account the mitigating factors in this case which are, firstly, your early guilty plea, and so full credit. Secondly, your age, 23, and no previous convictions, and everything I've heard about you indicates a bright future ahead and that this is a one-off that will never happen again. That provides mitigation. In my view this is so serious that custody is the only proper sentence, but giving credit I am prepared to suspend that, and make it clear that credit for guilt is in suspending. Sentence of the court will be fixed term imprisonment of 6 months, suspended for 2 years and you must understand that if you commit another offence during the course of the order or you breach the requirements you can expect prison to be activated and you'll go inside for 6 months. Additional requirements attached are 200 hours unpaid work to be completed within the next 12 months. In addition, a curfew at your home address from 7pm to 6am for 3 months.

Arguably in such cases deferring is of less utility then for an offender who has offended during periods of tumultuous personal circumstances, but who claims at sentencing that their lifestyle has been reformed. Deferral gives an opportunity to demonstrate that change. Where there has been no such change of circumstances, the offender is not in the same position of needing to demonstrate to the court that they can pass a period of time without committing further offences. Instead, the deterrent aspect comes from the threat of activation of the term of imprisonment.

---

66 Though note that the concept of a custody threshold is not universally supported – Padfield argues it gives a false sense of security by implying clarity where there is no exact threshold to be crossed, implies an unnecessary rigidity in the hierarchy of sentencing options which can mislead sentencers, and should be discarded: Padfield, N. (2011) Time to bury the custody threshold?, *Criminal Law Review*, 8, pp. 593–612.

67 *R v CF*, Camberwell Green Magistrates' Court, 11th May 2016.

When sentencing a young asylum seeker, NA, for a joint enterprise robbery in Central London, the Judge's frustration that an SSO imposed on NA the month before that offence, for assaulting an emergency worker, had not deterred him from committing the robbery, was clear:[68]

> NA, you had received an SSO in September 2019, that was to last for a year. You didn't wait a year before committing another offence; you didn't even wait one month! Showing total disregard to the criminal justice system in this country and a poor attitude towards the community.

For some offenders, there is a limit to the support that the criminal justice system can put in place to help them address the criminogenic factors in their lives. An example is DH. The Probation Officer explained in an oral report delivered at court that DH was engaging with the requirements of a CO that he was already under at the time of the offence, but that there were no other requirements that the Probation Service could offer him. As he was homeless, treatment options such as a Drug Rehabilitation Requirement were not suitable. The Judge sentenced him thus, for two charges of assault by beating, and two charges of failing to surrender to the court:[69]

> I heard this trial last week. The complainant was a vulnerable person and you went into her home and you really breached her trust in the way you behaved. I dismissed two charges but found you guilty of assaulting her before her friend RS left and afterwards when he got back. There were no significant injuries that I could be sure about but there were some. The record of your previous convictions and the fact that this was a very vulnerable person means that this offence crosses the custody threshold. But given that these are, in context of your life, old offences I'm going to suspend it. So I give you 8 weeks concurrent on each. For the Bail Act offence you receive 2 weeks consecutive. That is all suspended for 12 months. You have already got a package of community sentence requirements and that is the main thing supporting you. This hangs over you now, so any new offence in next 12 months and these weeks will be served.

In other cases, however, there is progress being made by the defendant of their own volition, which the court feels able to accept as an indicator that the offender has taken steps to reduce the likelihood of their committing

---

68 *R v BA and NA*, Southwark Crown Court, 17th September 2020.
69 *R v DH*, Reading Magistrates' Court, 6th February 2017.

further offences – whilst not deterrence, the aim of a reduction in crime is nonetheless being met, and the element of punishment is clear in the attachment of requirements. This may be especially forceful and persuasive in the context of an offender who has had previous periods of imprisonment that have not led them to desist from crime. Take the example of AG, who had assaulted his sister whilst on holiday at a static caravan site:[70]

> We have heard, Mr G, everything that has been said in court today by your solicitor,[71] by probation and by the Prosecution. This was a very nasty attack. It was sustained punches, you chased your sister and you knocked her to the ground and you hit her. Other people were present and you were under the influence. This is what we could class as a Category 1 offence [on the Sentencing Guidelines] and we're looking at custody. However, having read the pre-sentence report and listened to what the Probation Service and your solicitor said today, in terms of measures put in place to address drug addiction and negative drug samples, we are going to step back from custody; you've had small stretches inside and they haven't worked. For assault you'll receive 12 weeks' custody, consecutive to existing sentence. We are going to suspend this for 18 months. No requirements. A lot being put in at the moment to help you and you are now starting to turn up to the appointments.

Conclusion

Within sentencing provisions, reduction in crime and deterrence are portrayed as intrinsically linked to one another. However, this need not be the case, with deterrence being avoidance encouraged by the expectation of fear or pain on performing the prohibited activity – a process. Meanwhile a reduction in crime is an outcome, and one which can, as explored in the following chapters, be secured in many ways, a key one of which is rehabilitation. The often-portrayed-as-intrinsic link between punishment and deterrence is also lacking – whilst punishment may lead to deterrence, that link is not assured, and, as noted above, neither is it the exclusive route.

70 *R v AG*, Worthing Magistrates' Court, 9th February 2017.
71 I was appearing for the defendant, but many benches assume that everyone appearing in front of them is a solicitor, as opposed to a barrister.

3 Sentencing as rehabilitation

> Rehabilitation: Improvement of the character, skills, and behaviour of an offender through training, counselling, education, etc., in order to aid reintegration into society.
>
> (Oxford English Dictionary)

This chapter stands in part opposition, part reinforcement to the previous chapter, offering rehabilitation as both the opposite of punishment, and yet also something that can serve as punishment itself, or be a benefit to both the convicted individual, and the whole community, that flows from punishment.

Rehabilitation might not be the first thing that is thought of when considering sentencing in the criminal justice system. However, as criminological understanding of the reasons underlying offending have improved, the number of ways in which rehabilitation can be offered through sentencing has also increased.

A significant criticism of rehabilitation featuring at the sentencing stage could be that it does not feature any earlier in the process – by the point of sentencing the defendant already has a criminal conviction. Whilst the consequent help to tackle drug or alcohol misuse or mental health conditions might be welcome and effective, offenders are nonetheless going to experience the collateral consequences of a (or further) criminal conviction(s). When considering programmes offenders may engage in after conviction, there is research to show that even simply completing a programme may have a positive effect on reducing recidivism.[1] It is a shame that the current system only considers providing that chance once there has been a conviction, as opposed to a recognised route to diversion away from the offending which results in a conviction.

---

1 E.g. Hollin, C. R. and Palmer, E. J. (2009) Cognitive skills programmes for offenders, *Psychology, Crime & Law*, 15(2), pp. 147–164.

DOI: 10.4324/9781003201625-3

Deferred sentences

Something similar to such a model is already at work later in the sentencing process, chiefly through the possibility of a deferred sentence, as referred to in the previous chapter. Deferred sentences have been available for many years; currently in s.3 of the Sentencing Act 2020,[2] allowing the court to defer passing sentence for up to six months from the date of deferment (s.5(2)). The rationale is to allow the court to have regard to the conduct of the defendant after conviction (s.3(1)(a)), and the impact on them of any change in circumstances (s.3(1)(b)).

Section 2(2) permits the imposition of requirements as to the defendant's conduct during the period of the deferment, and their compliance with them will also be considered when the Judge comes to pass sentence on the date to which it is deferred (s.6(2)(a)). This can include a condition of residence (s.3(3)(a)). Whilst the period of deferment can include monitoring by an officer of a provider of probation services (s.8(1)(a)), due to its short duration it is not possible for an offender to undertake courses through the Probation Service. There is nothing to stop an offender seeking out private or NHS-provided treatment for matters such as addictions, anger management, counselling, or other support to demonstrate a commitment to addressing underlying criminogenic factors. The court could, alternatively, appoint someone other than an officer of a provider of probation services to supervise the offender – any other person whom the court thinks fit and who consents (s.8(1)(b)). Whether the person appointed is from the local probation board or elsewhere, they are under a duty to monitor the offender's compliance with the requirements (s.8(2)(a)) and, on the date of the deferred sentencing, to provide the court with information of the offender's compliance with the requirements (s.8(2)(b)).

Demonstrating an element of agency in the process, a sentence can only be deferred if the defendant consents (s.5(1)(a)). The other requirements are that the offender undertakes to comply with any requirements as to his conduct during the period of the deferment that the court considers it appropriate to impose (s.5(1)(b)), and the court is satisfied, having regard to the nature of the offence and the character and circumstances of the offender, that it would be in the interests of justice to exercise the power (s.5(1)(d)).

Reflecting the importance of abiding by the requirements that the offender has agreed to, and the role, albeit a subservient one, of deterrence even within apparently rehabilitative sentencing tools, a breach of any requirement has serious consequences. The court that deferred sentence may deal

---

2 Formerly s.1 of the Powers of Criminal Courts (Sentencing) Act 2000.

with the offender before the date to which sentence was deferred if the court is satisfied that the offender has failed to comply with one or more requirements imposed under the deferment (s.9(3)(b)); if the person supervising the offender (as described above) reports to the court that the offender has failed to comply with any of the requirements (s.9(1)(b));[3] or if the offender commits any offence in *Great Britain* (s.10(2)).[4]

Deferment allows the court to give an offender 'a second chance'. As noted above, the ship has sailed as regards conviction – the defendant cannot avoid the finding or admission of guilt. However, it allows a defendant to mitigate the effect of their wrongdoing on themselves through a reduced sentence. Anecdotally, the power to defer is often used where a defendant is young, has a very limited criminal record, or a gap in their offending suggesting a real attempt to desist, and could avoid immediate imprisonment if they co-operate with the requirements imposed. That this is implicitly supported by the legislation is apparent from s.5(4), which forbids a court deferring sentence to remand the defendant in custody – they need to be free in the community to demonstrate that they can resist offending behaviour triggers. Attached requirements need not be criminal justice–focussed, though a common one is to require no further criminal offences of any kind during the deferral.

The Crime and Courts Act 2013 inserted a further section (s.1ZA) into PCC(S)A 2000, now enshrined in s.7 of the Sentencing Act 2020, which placed a greater focus on the possibility of using deferred sentences in conjunction with restorative justice.[5] Restorative justice is explored in Chapter 5.

Two examples from my practice are apposite: both for young men whose cases had been significantly delayed within the criminal justice system, which meant that the lengthy time lapse from the offence to the date they were expecting to be sentenced had enabled them to demonstrate a capacity to stay out of trouble.

The first defendant was DC, discussed in the previous chapter.[6] He drove dangerously in April 2018. By the time his case was listed in the Crown Court, where he pleaded guilty, it was January 2020. In that intervening time he had not committed any further offences, in contrast to consistent offending between 2009 and the offence in April 2018.

---

3 In either circumstance that court has the power to either issue a summons, or a warrant for the offender's arrest – s.9(2)(a) and (b).

4 As per s.10(3)(a) and (b) – an interesting specification that this particular section includes offences committed in Scotland.

5 A restorative justice requirement (s.7) can be imposed if all parties – including the defendant and the victim – consent to it (s.7(2)).

6 *R v DC*, St Albans Crown Court, 27th February 2020.

Almost six months later, the case was back before the Judge for sentencing. The defendant had not only committed no further offences, but had managed to secure, and maintain, paid work, even during the national lockdown necessitated by the coronavirus pandemic. It is not possible, of course, to say that the deferred sentence had 'worked' – DC had already stayed out of trouble for over a year before the deferment. Rather, one perspective would be that the deferment gave DC a chance to demonstrate that change's longevity – that he was effectively rehabilitated through maturing and other changes in his life, and that therefore he did not need the criminal justice system to impose further strictures to direct him there. This led to him receiving a suspended sentence:

> You fall to be sentenced today for two offences, both date from 17.4.18. Facts can be shortly put – police endeavoured to stop you and a number of others on mopeds; you attempted to evade them, driving off extremely dangerously. I saw the CCTV footage of this several months ago and your riding was plainly extremely dangerous and alarming, putting yourself and members of the public going about their daily business, as your father or sister might have been, at significant risk. When you were in front of me I pointed to the wholly unacceptable delay in bringing these proceedings to court. Almost universal practice when someone has driven dangerously to try to evade police – I always put those people straight inside. I didn't purely because of the entirely unreasonable delay in bringing these proceedings, which I still don't understand. [...]
>
> It did for you represent a stroke of luck as what I was told about you on that day, and that you have kept out of trouble except a small drugs matter in April 2019, has shown you can keep out of trouble, can avoid the people you were hanging around with previously who were likely to lead you into trouble, and can earn a lawful wage. I still have to pass a sentence appropriate for what was, even over 2 years ago, a serious offence. For reasons set out, dangerous driving is always serious.
>
> [...] As I said back in February, the risk I was taking, the chance I was taking in deferring, we can see how that played out and you have done what I asked of you. You have stayed out of trouble and, in a time when work very difficult to find, you have worked through that period.
>
> This case crosses the custody threshold but I am not going to send you to prison today. I am going to give you an SSO – considerably shorter than it might otherwise have been. Short sentences, even hanging over someone's head, are often not a good idea. Judges are reminded that very little can be achieved in custodial setting when they are there for only a short time. Someone like you, I hope that with the threat of custody hanging over your head will remind you if you need it to stay

on the straight and narrow. [...]. You have demonstrated over two years that you can keep out of trouble.

Once again, the sentencing remarks by the Judge on this occasion show various aspects of s.57 in action, with the acknowledgement of deterrence, and alluding to the fact that the criminal behaviour as seen in April 2018 caused a risk that the public was entitled to be protected from.

The second deferment example is SR,[7] who had pleaded guilty to possession of Class A drugs with intent to supply. The offence was committed at the end of December 2018. Although he had previous convictions, including some committed in breach of SSOs, he had never been imprisoned. His sentence hearing fell during the strictest coronavirus lockdown.

The Judge observed as follows about his proposed course;

> I have no confidence today that he will keep his nose clean as he has a track record of misbehaving and ignoring court orders. I am conscious we are in the middle of a national crisis, I am conscious that he is now older by two years, I am conscious of the passage of time and I hope the penny is beginning to drop that if he carries on abusing drugs he is simply going to wreck the rest of his life and spend the rest of his life in and out of prison. If in 6 months' time he comes back and has complied with the objectives of the deferred sentence identified then I am likely to be merciful and lenient on that occasion.

The Judge then set out for the defendant how this leniency would be exhibited:

> On the Sentencing Guidelines, [...] 39 months – that is what you would receive today. Before I can suspend it must come down to 2 years, so you have got to prove to me that I should take a risk with you and my own reputation and pass a 2 year sentence on you and suspend it when I should be sending you to prison for 39 months.

Pointing out that he had seen SR's recent conviction for drink driving (committed since the offence for which he was being sentenced), the Judge set five objectives:

1   No further offending of any sort
2   No drugs
3   Keep down a job and provide evidence of doing so

7 *R v SR*, Wood Green Crown Court, 15th May 2020.

4   Keep in touch with Probation Service
5   Obtain voluntary drug treatment

He continued;

> If by 20th November, and I expect report from Probation Service, I am told he has kept all of those five objectives I will give you a sentence of 2 years suspended for 2 years with 200 hours unpaid work plus any treatment programmes then felt to be necessary. If I am told that you have let me down in any one of those five objectives you will go to prison for 39 months.

At the deferred sentence hearing, SR did not attend. He was in police custody, having been charged with a new offence of possession with intent to supply of Class A drugs, and was awaiting his first appearance before the magistrates' court. SR later pleaded guilty to that new offence, meaning he had breached the deferment by further offending.

Arguably in both of these cases the initial step towards desistance has been taken by the defendants themselves. However, considering the known criminogenic effect of imprisonment, deferring sentence gives a Judge a meaningful way to support a defendant who is already taking steps to move away from offending. By waiting to sentence them for a period of up to six months to see if those steps can continue, a deferred sentence allows a route for the monitoring and encouragement of rehabilitation above and beyond mere desistance from criminal activity. For DC, this paid off. For SR, the outcome was less positive.

A slightly different example is that of ML,[8] aged 39. He had pleaded guilty to acquisitive offending from two supermarkets within a day, and making off from a restaurant without paying the following week. The two thefts from supermarkets were committed the day after he received an SSO for two offences of theft from the previous year. All these offences were committed to fund his alcohol addiction. His sentence was deferred for three months – from April to July. The requirements set out by the Judge were:

> The purpose of this deferment is to enable the Court to have regard to:
>
> 1   Your conduct after conviction and before sentence.
> 2   Your use of the opportunity to repay the victims of the thefts and making off without payment offences and produce a receipt that can be verified by the police.

8 *R v ML*, St Albans Crown Court, 12th July 2018.

3   Your use of the opportunity to demonstrate that you are abstaining from alcohol and are attending counselling for alcohol addiction

4   Your use of the opportunity to obtain gainful employment.

In light of your breach of the suspended sentence the Court will expect substantial achievement if an immediate prison sentence is to be avoided.

Even this shorter deferment period was sufficient for ML to substantially reduce his drinking, which was seen to be a sufficient effort to give the Judge confidence that eventually ML would abstain altogether, and that he only committed criminal offences when he was in drink. The Judge there-fore imposed another SSO of one month's imprisonment suspended for nine months, and compensation to the three victim companies:

ML, I deferred sentence on 18th April and I gave you a number of requirements for you to meet before I sentenced you and it's clear from what I have seen and heard that you took that seriously and have made efforts to address the position. You have endeavoured to repay the victims although that has not met with success for understandable reasons.[9] You have made use of the opportunity to demonstrate that you are endeavour-ing to become free of alcohol and attending counselling for your alcohol addiction. It is extremely important that you understand that recognising the problem is crucial. You will understand eventually that you cannot drink at all. Coming down to one to two pints a day is an achievement but reality is you can't drink. At the end of today there will be a substan-tial custodial sentence if you further offend and the only way I see you offending is if you drink. [You fall to be sentenced today for] Theft from two shops, making off without paying, and breach of an SSO imposed on the 10th May at Luton Crown Court when the Judge gave you a very real chance, for a serious offence. The reaction you had was to go off the rails immediately, and go out on a stealing spree. I am prepared to make allowance for the fact that these offences were to feed that habit.

There is mitigation that I have seen[10] and you have told me about detox; you have a residential course pending and I would strongly

9   ML was unrepresented and when he had contacted the shops concerned seeking to pay them compensation, none of them had known how he could go about that. He had pro-duced at court various emails he had sent trying to find the right person to contact, and the responses he had received which did not answer his questions.

10 Documents had been provided to the Judge at court.

counsel that you take that course and take it seriously. The documents satisfy me so that I am sure that you have met the requirement for employment and you should have credit for that. Alcohol is the root course of your offending. The SSO help had no time to take effect before new offences.[11]

Rehabilitation is often a pre-eminent feature of SSOs. As the Judge noted in the sentencing comments above, the earlier SSO that had been imposed had not had time to have a positive effect on ML prior to him committing further offences. However, by the deferred sentence hearing, a report from the offender manager supervising his pre-existing SSO showed that he was engaging well with unpaid work and the rehabilitative requirements focussed on his alcohol addiction.

Community sentences and rehabilitation

Where an offender has addictions which they recognise as contributing to their offending, many courts consider that the best way to tackle that underlying criminogenic issue is intervention in the community, whether through an SSO, or, where the offence does not cross the custody threshold, a CO.

When sentencing JB for being in charge of a motor vehicle with a blood alcohol content significantly above the drink-drive limit, the bench cited her efforts in already seeking help with her alcohol problem as significant to their sentencing decision:[12]

> We give you full credit for your early guilty plea, and we have taken into account the things said on your behalf, and that you are attending alcohol treatment of your own volition. But this is an incredibly high reading, one of the highest this court has seen. The engine was running, the car door was open and you were in the driving seat. You were so incoherent you couldn't communicate with police. People were ringing up [the police] as [they were] so concerned. We notice you have a failure to provide a sample in 2013, and this adds to this offence as it is not your first time in court. We recognise you have an alcohol problem. We impose a 12-month Community Order with 100 hours unpaid work.

SSOs and COs are also recognised by Judges as providing a meaningful way for offenders to be supported by the Probation Service to address

---

11 As the SSO had only been imposed the day before the current offences, and so ML had had no intervention from probation yet.
12 *R v JB*, Highbury Corner Magistrates' Court, 13th July 2016.

factors underlying their offending, and thus facilitate rehabilitation. Aside from direct interventions on issues such as drugs and alcohol, supervision by the Probation Service can also have a much more general value.

Take, for example, JF,[13] who was being sentenced for breaching an SSO that had been imposed when she had only narrowly avoided immediate custody after making threats to kill to one of her children, assaulting another, and assaulting the arresting officer. The breach then occurred when, drunk, she assaulted two police officers sent to remove her from a train.

In sentencing her to a CO for the new offences, and adding further Rehabilitation Activity Requirement days to her original SSO for the breach, the Judge observed:

> I am dealing with the breach by way of 20 RAR days added to the suspended sentence order taking them to a maximum of 60. I can't extend the term [operational period] as it's the maximum already. There are 9 months left on it, so if you re-offend in the next 9 months that would be the second breach and then it'd be difficult not to send you to prison.
>
> I'm not sending you to prison but you need to be under the care or attention of the Probation Service for longer than the 9 months left on the SSO, so I'm giving you an 18-month Community Order so you will have a person at Probation Service responsible for your management and they will deal with any problems arising from your conduct.

This demonstrates the value recognised by many Judges in the Probation Service's work with offenders to support them in avoiding triggers for their offending behaviour, and that such work is often supportive and guidance-led. Indeed this may explain why so many offenders who engage with probation note that their personal relationship with a probation officer, who demonstrates genuine interest in their lives and wellbeing, has the greatest impact on their rehabilitation.[14]

As seen in the example above, for offenders who have drug or alcohol addictions, these are often linked to their commission of offences. A key step to their effective rehabilitation is often the ending of that dependency. Some offenders have already sought that help before they are sentenced, and courts can be alive to reflecting this in their eventual sentence. For example, YM was already engaging in such a programme, having pleaded

---

13 *R v JF*, Chelmsford Crown Court, 31th August 2016.
14 Weaver, B. and McNeill, F. (2010) 'Travelling hopefully: Desistance Research and Probation Practice'. In: J. Brayford, F. Cowe, and J. Deering (eds) What Else Works?: Creative Work with Offenders. Cullompton: Willan; pp. 36–60.

guilty to assaulting a shop worker and then obstructing a police officer in the execution of his duty, both of which happened whilst she was heavily intoxicated:[15]

> We've been looking at two charges to which you've pleaded guilty, of common assault and obstructing a P.C. For the common assault, using our guidelines we go through the offences to find whether they are more or less serious. We've decided lesser harm and lower culpability as lack of premeditation, so lowest category. But what makes more serious is your previous convictions for similar, and they all involve alcohol, as did this. The person you assaulted was a public servant, working in a supermarket, and you spat at him. What makes it less serious is that it was an isolated incident, and you expressed remorse about the police officers. This takes the offences to a low Community Order but we consider your circumstances, and we note that you are seeking treatment voluntarily for alcohol and mental health issues, which is to your credit, and we think this should continue. You must continue with this. The Community Order threshold has been passed but we are going to deal with this by way of financial penalties to reflect your guilty plea.'

In their 2017 Report Mental Health and Fair Trial, JUSTICE noted that where an offender had mental health problems, it was particularly likely that victims would support a medical intervention that was aimed at assisting the offender with improving their mental health.[16] Such a suggestion had been raised nearly ten years earlier by Lord Bradley in his 2009 Report.[17]

JUSTICE used, in support of their suggestion that this approach would be approved by complainants, a report published by Victim Support in 2010,[18] which highlighted that victims needed a greater understanding of sentencing. This is supported by existing academic research which highlights that most members of the public know very little about sentencing and how it

15 *R v YM*, Aylesbury Magistrates' Court, 13th May 2016.
16 JUSTICE (2017) Mental Health and Fair Trial, London: JUSTICE, at para 2.10 https://ju stice.org.uk/wp-content/uploads/2017/11/JUSTICE-Mental-Health-and-Fair-Trial-Report -2.pdf [accessed 25th October 2020].
17 The Bradley Report (2009) Executive Summary, London: Department of Health, p. 4, para 16 https://bulger.co.uk/prison/Dept-of-Health-Bradley-Report-Exec-Summary.pdf [accessed 25th October 2020].
18 Victim Support (2010) Victims' justice? What victims and witnesses really want from sentencing, London: Victim Support, pp. 16–17 www.victimsupport.org.uk/sites/default/files/ Victims%27%20justice%20-%20What%20victims%20and%20witnesses%20really%2 0want%20from%20sentencing.pdf [accessed 25th October 2020].

works in practice.[19] Although many make generalised complaints about the leniency of sentences,[20] when they are given the specific facts of a scenario and asked what they think would be an appropriate sentence, they were most likely to propose a sentence not dissimilar to that actually imposed by the sentencing Judge.[21]

Where someone has taken steps to address the root cause of their offending behaviour even before sentence, the court may be able to suspend a sentence of imprisonment as they can have confidence that the reduction of crime (see Chapter 2) will have been addressed by the offender taking steps to tackle the underlying causes of their criminal behaviour. An example was LR, who drank to cope with post-traumatic stress disorder arising from childhood sexual abuse, an acrimonious marriage breakdown, and a child-custody battle:[22]

> What led to the offence itself is significant enough, and your personal circumstances add to that. The efforts and actions that you have taken by getting professional support that you need not only to address those emotional factors but also to ensure that you don't commit offences and don't come back to court. Because of this we can suspend that custody for a period of 12 months and we do.

For many, despite significant attempts by the system to provide opportunities for rehabilitation, the courts are a revolving door – no sooner have they served one sentence, they are committing new offences, as with JM:[23]

> You have a long record of offending. You are aged 41, you have 33 convictions for 97 offences. It is a long, sad and familiar record. Much of it burglary or other acquisitive offending. It resulted in sentencing by me last December of just under 5 years – 4 years 10 months – for a series of burglaries and other offences committed before and after the current offences I am dealing with today. Those were burglaries and assault on a constable. That sentence was the culmination of a long history of offending including 3 years imprisonment for robbery in 2015. There's not much the courts can do as you've had, over

19 Roberts, J. V. and Hough, M. (2005), 'Understanding public attitudes to criminal justice', (London: Open University Press).
20 Hough, M. et al. (2009), 'Research report 6: public attitudes to the principles of sentencing', Sentencing Advisory Panel – see further details in the Introduction.
21 *Ibid*, at pp. 61–62.
22 *R v LR*, Colchester Magistrates Court, 17th February 2017.
23 *R v JM*, Luton Crown Court, 13th February 2018.

the years, all sorts of sentencing – suspended, community; attempts to rehabilitate you and until you decide that you don't want to spend time in prison for the rest of your life I expect that this will continue. The motivation to change has to come from you.

The need for an offender to take ownership and control over their future to facilitate rehabilitation is of such importance that there are require-ments that can be attached to a CO or SSO that require the consent of the offender before they can be imposed. These are mental health treatment requirements and alcohol and drug treatment requirements. The need for consent demonstrates a recognition of what the Judge was communicating to JM – that rehabilitation is a process dependent not just upon the services being available, but also the offender wanting to engage with those services. Rehabilitation cannot be imposed upon someone.

JK provoked a Judge's frustration by his failure to engage with a PSR, which might have meant that a less harsh sentence could have been imposed, and his failure to provide evidence of claimed self-rehabilitating. What's more, he had been given an SSO after the date of commission of the current offences for other unrelated offences, and there was material from the Probation Service that suggested that he was not complying with that Order either:[24]

When you were searched at the police station, in your shorts' pocket you had two bladed articles – a Stanley knife blade and a craftwork blade. Both were unsheathed and unaccompanied by any form of tool. So far as that is concerned you've admitted you were in possession and you pleaded guilty. You explained the articles generally were had for work purposes but you had forgotten that they were in your shorts' pocket. That is hard to believe in terms of what they weigh and the risk of you putting your hand in [and suffering a cut from them]. But you admitted they were there and yours.

As far as my sentencing is concerned, you say that you are a man doing his best to re-order his family life and set up work. You have failed to attend for PSR appointments, putting forward that you're at work, but you have failed to provide any evidence [of being at work]. Equally when it comes to the SSO (imposed on 26/7/16) that you are not in breach of, a report suggests that you are unco-operative and on the verge of being breached. That doesn't sound to me like someone who is trying to get their life together. You have a poor record for acquisitive crime but no offences regarding weapons or their use, and therefore I treat you in this sense as a man without a history in relation to possession of weapons.

As far as these offences are concerned, if you had co-operated with the pre-sentence procedure, it is possible that I would have been persuaded that some form of Community Order was appropriate. I cannot pass that as you have not put yourself in a position for me to do so. I am urged to impose a fine but I have concerns as to the source of funds due to your previous offending and a lack of confirmatory material as to where your income comes from. However, as you have an SSO that you have yet to be breached for; passed only 4 days after this offence was committed, I have been persuaded not to send you immediately into custody; though you could not have made it more likely if you had tried.

These sentences reflect that I am unable to pass a Community Order due to your lack of co-operation in community service. I give you credit for guilty pleas.

It is striking that the Judge is very clear that had JK co-operated with the Probation Service to assess his suitability for a CO through a PSR, then the Judge might have been able to find that the offence did not cross the custody threshold, and to impose a non-custodial sentence – as opposed to simply non-immediate custody. In that respect a CO would have carried a lower risk of imprisonment (it not being the presumptive result of breach) than the SSO that the Judge felt had to be imposed.

Something not always acknowledged about the criminal justice system, though there is much criminological research on its importance,[25] is that rehabilitation is rarely a process that takes place in isolation and without assistance, albeit that it is rooted in the offender's own desire for change and a move away from offending.[26] Sometimes it is support that offenders are missing, and its absence can be influential in offenders' struggles to

---

25 There is far too much research on this to give a comprehensive list, but a few examples include: Sampson and Laub's theory of desistance which revolves around life events such as marriage; Sampson, R. J. and Laub, J. H. (2005) A life course view of the development of crime, *Annals of the American Academy of Political and Social Science*, 602, pp. 12–45; and research on the role of friends, social and peer groups: Giordano, P., Cernkovich, S., and Holland, D. (2003) Changes in friendship relations over the life course: implications for desistance from crime, *Criminology*, 41, p. 293.

26 Maruna, S. and Roy, K. (2007) Amputation or Reconstruction? Notes on the Concept of 'Knifing Off' and Desistance From Crime', *Journal of Contemporary Criminal Justice*, 23(1), pp. 104–124.

desist from criminal behaviour. So common can the absence of support be, that some sentencing Judges are genuinely surprised when it is clearly in evidence in the life of a person whom they are sentencing, as for LC:[27]

> I am not going to impose an immediate custodial sentence, though one is not at all unusual for offences of attempted robbery. Your behaviour on this occasion was out of character, but truly appalling. The fact that you don't remember it and were on drugs at the time doesn't in any way reduce the impact that your appalling conduct had on your victim. You tried to rob him – punched him, and entirely understandable that he was somebody who had suffered as a result of your appalling behaviour. You are only 19, and this offence is a serious escalation of those in the past, but it is entirely out of character. As counsel has said and as is clear, your mother is here to support you and that is not at all usual in 19 year old young men who appear before this court. Many do not come with their mothers or anybody at all and the fact that your mother is here and you are supported by your family makes this an unusual case and shows you have the support of your family. In addition, unlike many young men appearing before this court, who appear incapable of, and unwilling to get, a job, you are somebody who, I see from certificates, has impressive certificates and also in recent days have tried to get employment. I hope that you succeed. So in the light of all that I know about you, all that's in the PSR, I do have to impose a custodial sentence, but one that I am going to suspend.

However, despite general ideological support, rehabilitation is not necessarily 'built in' to all sentence types in the way it is encouraged in SSOs and COs. For example, mandatory minimum sentences, which require that for specific types of offences offenders serve no less than a period specified in statute, and the sort of rehabilitation (or lack thereof) that offenders receive once they are in prison, are wholly outside the influence of Judges who are passing sentence. Therefore, one significant barrier to rehabilitation in the English criminal justice system is that after sentence, the rehabilitative options provided are not necessarily what the Judge who was sentencing envisioned. Perhaps even more problematic is the timescale which it might take to receive that rehabilitative assistance. One type of sentence which illustrated the challenges of detaining someone in prison until they are judged to have been rehabilitated was the Imprisonment for Public Protection ('IPP') sentence.

---

27 *R v LC*, Southwark Crown Court, 24th January 2020.

Imprisonment for Public Protection – 'IPP'

This sentence type was introduced in 2005, in the same legislation as the aims and objectives of sentences that give the structure to this book: the Criminal Justice Act 2003. From a theoretical standpoint it was a paradigm example of how multiple aims and objectives could be given effect within one sentence type – imprisonment to protect the public in the short-term, whilst simultaneously rehabilitating so that the public continue to be protected on the offender's release.

IPP's main rationale was protection, as evident from the name. The Halliday Report into sentencing in 2001 highlighted that there was no coherent way of dealing with sexual and violent offenders, hindering the monitoring of progress during their sentence, and maintenance of supervisory contact on their release.[28] Consequently,[29] the CJA 03 provided for the first time a specific sentence for 'dangerous offenders'. The Criminal Justice and Immigration Act 2008 ('CJIA 08'), tempered the CJA 03 with amendments to make IPP discretionary instead of mandatory.

IPP sentences fit both here, and in Chapter 4 on protection. For cohesion, most discussion is centred in this chapter. Underpinning IPP was that if an offender's imprisonment was indeterminate, then their release would not be according to an arbitrary timetable – once they had served half of the sentence, calculated on the basis of the harm and culpability of their original offence, but with no forward-looking considerations. Instead, release would be granted once the prisoner had (a) served their tariff period,[30] and (b) been adjudged by the Parole Board as safe to be released back into society – 'rehabilitated'. This might seem an appealing rationale – it is not suggested that it is theoretically wanting, but the practice was regrettably different.

IPP was abolished in 2012. In its seven-year lifespan it was the subject of numerous appeals, and some of those who received it remain in prison in 2021, nine years after its abolition, and in some cases, 16 years since they were imprisoned.

---

28 Halliday, J. (2001) *Making Punishments Work: Report of a Review Of The Sentencing Framework For England And Wales* ('The Halliday Report'), Chapter 4.

29 Explanatory Notes to the Criminal Justice Act 2003, Chapter 44 www.legislation.gov.uk/ukpga/2003/44/pdfs/ukpgaen_20030044_en.pdf [accessed 25th October 2020].

30 This was the minimum length of sentence that the offender could serve – that period judged to correspond to the determinate sentence for the offence committed, calculated on the basis of the seriousness of the offence, which is calculated by reference to the harm caused and the offender's culpability for it.

How to get rehabilitated (and prove it)

The CJA 03 allowed that a prisoner serving an IPP sentence would be released when they were no longer a risk to the public as defined by s.225(1) (b). That requires the offender to satisfy the Parole Board that they no longer pose such a risk – the sticking point is how can they achieve this.

The idea was that by undertaking courses available in custody, appropriately targeted at behaviours or personality characteristics causing or related to their offending, a prisoner could reduce their risk and demonstrate this reduction to the Parole Board, through reports from course administrators and their own attitudinal change.

Unfortunately, the rehabilitative aims were not matched by the availability of programmes across prisons. Consequently, many IPP prisoners became 'trapped' in prison awaiting courses. Some courses were not available at their prison; others were available, but short-term prisoners were given priority. As those serving IPP 'weren't going anywhere' there was no incentive to prioritise them for programmes with high demand and limited supply.

This unsatisfactory situation caused two IPP prisoners to bring legal proceedings against the Secretary of State for Justice.[31] The Court encountered:[32]

> the consequences of the fact that the provisions of the CJA 2003 have resulted in more offenders in need of rehabilitation being imprisoned than existing resources can accommodate.

David Walker ('DW') had been sentenced to IPP with a minimum term of 18 months for two indecent assaults; Brett James ('BJ') to IPP with a minimum term of one year and 295 days for wounding with intent, both under the original CJA 03 formulation of IPP. Both men were at HMP Doncaster, a Serco-run private prison. BJ had served his minimum term at the time of the hearing, DW had not. Consequently the Court of Appeal took slightly different stances towards each, as explored below.

In 2005, Her Majesty's Chief Inspector of Prisons ('HMCIP') had identified that the enhanced Thinking Skills Programme ('TSP' – a common rehabilitative programme for offenders) had been withdrawn at HMP Doncaster

---

31 *Secretary of State for Justice v Walker and James* [2008] EWCA Civ 30; [2008] 1 W.L.R. 1977.

32 *Walker and James* as described by Phillips LCJ in *Brooke* [2008] EWCA Civ 29; [2008] 1 W.L.R. 1950 at [3]. The Lord Chief Justice sat on both the appeals of Walker and James, and Brooke.

due to costs, meaning there was no course provision for IPP prisoners,[33] which HMCIP recommended was rectified.

However, an unannounced inspection in 2008 highlighted that challenges facing IPP prisoners at HMP Doncaster had actually escalated – there were 20 IPP prisoners in 2005, 64 in 2008.[34] More pertinently for DW and BJ, there was still no TSP available.[35] DW had had 'no access to any meaningful programme, course or work' through which he could demonstrate to the Parole Board reduction in risk such that they could release him.[36] The Lord Chief Justice identified that:

> There has been a systemic failure on the part of the Secretary of State to put in place the resources necessary to implement the scheme of rehabilitation necessary to enable the relevant provisions of the 2003 Act to function as intended.[37]

For these reasons, the Court of Appeal held that the Secretary of State for Justice was in breach of his public law duty by failing to provide relevant offending behaviour courses to allow IPP prisoners to demonstrate to the Parole Board, within their tariff periods, that their imprisonment was no longer necessary for public protection. DW and BJ had been effectively denied review of their detention's lawfulness by not having their cases heard by the Parole Board. Continuation would likely result in breaching Article 5(4) of the European Convention on Human Rights ('ECHR'), which states that:

> Everyone who is deprived of his liberty by arrest or detention shall be entitled to take proceedings by which the lawfulness of his detention shall be decided speedily by a court and his release ordered if his detention is not lawful.

It is particularly notable that DW's situation was recorded by his Indeterminate Sentences Manager thus:

---

33 HMCIP (2005) Report on an announced inspection of HMP/YOI Doncaster (14–18 November 2005) by HM Chief Inspector of Prisons, at p. 69. The report is available at: https://webarchive.nationalarchives.gov.uk/20120405175937/http://www.justice.gov.uk/downloads/publications/hmipris/prison-and-yoi-inspections/doncaster/2005Doncaster-rps.pdf [accessed 23rd May 2021].

34 HMCIP (2008) Report on an unannounced full follow-up inspection of HMP/YOI Doncaster (11–15 February 2008) by HM Chief Inspector of Prisons, at p. 81.

35 *Ibid*, [8.13], p. 79.

36 [2008] EWCA Civ 30, at [24].

37 *Ibid*, at [70].

Although Mr Walker's custodial behaviour may justify transfer to open conditions or release, the fact that he has not as yet had his sentence plan or undertaken any work around relapse prevention would to my mind stand in the way of this.

DW's progress was barred not by his own behaviour, but the absence of hoops through which he needed to jump for release. The Court of Appeal held that DW and BJ's detention would cease to be justified under Art 5(1)(a) when it was no longer necessary for the protection of the public, or if so long elapsed without meaningful review that their detention became disproportionate or arbitrary. On the facts, that stage had not been reached.

On appeal to the House of Lords this broad principle was upheld. Unless an IPP prisoner was past their tariff period *and* could demonstrate their safety for release, their continued detention was not unlawful at common law, nor in breach of Art 5(4). Neither did it breach Art 5(1) unless there had been years without any effective review.[38]

The case was taken to the European Court of Human Rights ('ECtHR'),[39] by three applicants – Nicholas Wells ('NW'), Jeffrey Lee ('JL'), and Brett James. Similarly to both BJ and DW, NW and JL had been sentenced to 'short tariff' IPP sentences – NW for attempted robbery leading to IPP with a tariff of 12 months, less 58 days spent on remand, and JL for criminal damage. He was sentenced to IPP with a tariff of nine months, less time spent on remand. His tariff period therefore expired 163 days after sentence.

NW's offender manager observed that he had a better chance of accessing required programmes in the community on very strict release conditions; the programmes were not available in his current prison and the Prison Service would not transfer him. However, the Parole Board had noted:

Unfortunately it is not the remit of the Parole Board to make up for the deficiencies of the Prison Service. We are charged with a duty not to release life prisoners while their risk of serious offending remains high. Because you have not been able to do any of the appropriate courses you are unable to demonstrate any reduction in risk from the time of your sentence. Because your risk remains high, the Panel cannot direct your release as requested.[40]

The ECtHR held unanimously that there had been a violation of Art 5(1) in respect of the applicants' detention following the expiry of their tariff

---

38 *R(Wells) v Parole Board of England and Wales* [2009] UKHL 22.
39 *James, Wells and Lee v United Kingdom* (2013) 56 EHRR 12.
40 *Ibid*, at [49].

periods and until steps were taken to progress them through the prison system to provide them with access to appropriate rehabilitative courses. Consequently it unanimously ordered compensation to the Applicants. All other parts of the claim were dismissed.

This string of appellate case law demonstrates that even where an offender is sentenced in a way that could facilitate rehabilitation, it is not then within the Judge's power to ensure that such rehabilitation is offered, unless a specific requirement is attached to a CO or SSO, that is accepted and co-operated with by the offender.

At the end of March 2020,[41] there remained 1,969 serving IPP prisoners in England and Wales. Whilst that overall figure is a decrease of 15% in the last 12 months, it disguises two worrying rises. Firstly, the number of IPP prisoners recalled to custody after release increasing; in the preceding year the recalled IPP population had grown by 22% (to 1,359). Secondly, that the proportion of IPP prisoners who are post-tariff continued to increase – 94% of IPP prisoners as of 30th June 2020 compared to 92% a year earlier.

Furthermore, even eight years after its abolition, many prisoners serving IPP sentences have served multiples of their tariff period. As of 30th June 2020,[42] there were ten prisoners who had served 4,802 days (13.2 years) or more after their tariff period but before their first release from prison. The longest-serving such prisoner had served 5,223 days (14.3 years) over their tariff period before their initial release. High numbers of IPP prisoners still detained, past their tariff, and without access to courses enabling them to move through the system, is a perennial problem: in 2016, HMCIP published a thematic report entitled 'Unintended Consequences'.[43] It noted that 'rehabilitation' was given a very narrow interpretation – essentially amounting to a question of whether the prisoner had completed the 'correct' courses,[44] not all of which had rigorous quantitative evidence to demonstrate that they did in fact reduce an offender's risk and therefore protect the public on their release.[45]

41 www.gov.uk/government/publications/offender-management-statistics-quarterly-janu ary-to-march-2020--2/offender-management-statistics-quarterly-january-to-march-2020 [accessed 27th October 2020].

42 https://questions-statements.parliament.uk/written-questions/detail/2020-10-07/100343 [accessed 15th October 2020].

43 HM Inspectorate of Prisons (2016) Unintended consequences: Finding a way forward for prisoners serving sentences of imprisonment for public protection, Thematic Review, London: Her Majesty's Inspectorate of Prison.

44 See 'Unintended Consequences', paras 5.37, 5.38, 7.9, and www.gov.uk/guidance/offen ding-behaviour-programmes-and-interventions [accessed 15th October 2020].

45 This is part of a general reluctance on the part of the Government to commission and release independent research evaluations from randomised controlled trials of offender behaviour programmes – see e.g. Hollin, C. R. (2008) Evaluating offending behaviour

For those able to access courses and 'prove' their rehabilitation, they then had to wait increasingly long periods for a Parole Board hearing. The National Audit Office ('NAO') investigated the backlog of outstanding cases in 2008 and highlighted that the Parole Board could not cope with its own workload, and was also constrained by delays within other agencies with whom it had to work closely, such as the Ministry of Justice.[46] On further review in 2017,[47] there had been no improvement. The NAO highlighted that whilst the *Osborn* ruling in 2013[48] had increased the entitlement to an oral hearing to more prisoners, the Parole Board had not been able to proportionately increase its capacity to hear applications.[49] Despite restrictions necessitated by coronavirus in 2020, the Chair of the Parole Board stated that the backlog of cases awaiting a hearing date had reduced by 46%.[50]

Without solutions to these issues, the outlook for remaining IPP prisoners is bleak. The Legal Aid, Sentencing and Punishment of Offenders Act 2012 ('LASPOA') allowed a glimmer of hope – it included s.128, allowing the Secretary of State to change the test for release of IPP prisoners. However, nine years later, this has not been done, and there is no indication that it will be.

Conclusion

IPP has provided a salutary lesson in the need to approach not just the theoretical possibilities for rehabilitation, but to ensure that in practice there are the resources – in terms of funding, staff, and suitable prison places – to carry that ideal through to fruition. Whilst it is hard to disagree with the idea behind IPP, it is also hard to overstate the damaging effect of its reality for many offenders who received extremely short tariffs, only to become lodged in a system that would not help them to progress out of it. The danger with a system that requires an offender to 'earn' their way out of it by demonstrating attributes or changes can only function fairly if it gives

---

programmes: Does only randomization glister?, *Criminology and Criminal Justice*, 8(1), pp. 89–106.

46 Comptroller and Auditor General, Protecting the public: the work of the Parole Board, Session 2007–2008, HC 239, National Audit Office, March 2008.

47 Comptroller and Auditor General, Investigation into the Parole Board, Session 2016–2017, HC 1013, February 2017.

48 *Osborn v The Parole Board* [2013] UKSC 61.

49 Fn 46, at p. 4.

50 www.gov.uk/government/news/chief-executives-blog-parole-board-covid-19-recovery-plan [accessed 15th October 2020].

access to tools to facilitate that change, methods of assessing it, and opportunities to demonstrate it.

At lower levels of offending, however, rehabilitation is often easier to incorporate into a sentence, and can be crucial in its support of the second aim identified in s.57(2) – the reduction of crime. Its use within the system reflects the huge numbers of offenders whose offending stems from addictions to drink or drugs, or from mental ill-health – demonstrated by the significantly higher rates of a variety of mental health diagnoses and symptoms amongst prisoners than in the general population.[51] For many of these offenders, with appropriate professional help and support, the prospect of a law-abiding life is within reach. Rehabilitation can be expensive to administer, but many argue that it is an approach which pays back in the longer term by reducing recidivism rates more effectively than a model that seeks only to deter through punishment, as well as recognising agency and potential in offenders.

---

51 Durcan, G. (2016) Mental Health and Criminal Justice Report, *Centre for Mental Health*, London: Centre for Mental Health, p. 9.

4 Sentencing as protection

Within the criminal justice system there are four primary recipients of protection: the victim, potential future victims, society at large, and, in some instances, the defendant themselves.[1]

How these parties are protected by sentencing varies. As we saw in the introduction, the idea behind the application of the five aims and objectives in s.57(2) is that in conjunction with one another, they reduce future offending, thereby protecting all parties from the negative effects of offending behaviour. However, different methods of providing protection may have different reaches. For example, whilst imprisoning an offender will offer protection to society, including past and potential victims, from the offender for the term that they are imprisoned, if they are released without having been rehabilitated and/or without adequate supervision in the community,[2] then that protection is necessarily time-limited to the duration of their imprisonment. Similarly, reform (and consequent protection) is not the automatic result of punishment, as explored in Chapter 1.

After exploring why protection has to be considered when sentencing offenders, and how that consideration manifests, I suggest that there are two main ways in which a focus on protection appears in the criminal justice system currently – mandatory minimum sentences, and specific sentences for 'dangerous offenders'. Having explored its contribution to rehabilitation

---

1 For example, where a defendant is denied bail for their own protection whilst criminal proceedings are ongoing (under Schedule 1 of the Bail Act 1976), or the transfer of a psychiatrically unwell defendant to a psychiatric hospital for care under the powers in the Mental Health Act whilst they are remanded in custody (s.48 of the Mental Health Act 1983).
2 Much could be written about the effect of early release from prison and licence conditions on protection, but this book's focus is the use of the objectives in the sentencing process, and thus space precludes consideration of matters relating to release, something over which the sentencing Judge has no influence.

DOI: 10.4324/9781003201625-4

in Chapter 3, I also explore why, in the context of protection, IPP wreaked havoc on the criminal justice system in its short lifetime.

Protection from what?

Almost every criminal offence is predicated on the fact that harm is caused or risked through the prohibited behaviour. However, the exact type of harm, and the methods by which it is caused, vary hugely. Take, for example, the following two excerpts from sentencing remarks. The first concerns a case of possession of indecent images of children, for which DF, in his early 30s, of good character, was sentenced to an SSO of 13.5 months suspended for 18 months, with 60 days of a Rehabilitation Activity Requirement, plus a Sexual Harm Prevention Order ('SHPO').[3,4]

> It is important that you understand why these offences are taken so seriously by the courts. This is about the abuse of children, in this case, particularly young children. Just because you download and look does not mean you are not participating in the abuse of those children. By downloading and viewing you are a participant in the abuse of those children and that is why it is taken so seriously. I was troubled when I read the PSR that you are having difficulties with that insight. Minimising involvement and saying [you are] interested in young girls, but not prepubescent [girls], [that can't be true] given what you downloaded and the searching you were doing. [I note that you] accepted to [the probation officer] that you did understand that children who were being used were being harmed in the process. That is beginning of understanding of evil of this material, and you have started on the road of insight.

The second case is somewhat different; ML had been convicted after trial of possession with intent to supply of Class B drugs. He had a previous conviction for the same offence three years earlier, for which he had received ten months' imprisonment, plus convictions for simple drug possession (as opposed to the more serious offence of possession with intent to supply), which had resulted in fines and, in one case, a Community Order:[5]

> There is only one conclusion to the facts evident from this trial when read in the context of your previous convictions; you are a pedlar of

---

3 Imposed according to s.343 of the Sentencing Act 2020, formerly in s.103A of the Sexual Offences Act 2003 – this is a preventive order which can be made only where it is necessary for the purpose of protecting the public from a risk of sexual harm from the offender.

4 *R v DF*, Inner London Crown Court, 26th July 2018.

5 *R v ML*, St Albans Crown Court, 8th August 2017.

controlled drugs of Class B. You lied before this jury to conceal the trail that inexorably led to your door and your conviction. When you were stopped in Dec 2016 by PC B, and that was a good piece of work on his behalf, you had mobiles bearing all of the texts showing you were dealing that day. On 18th there was a whole series of texts on one of those dirty phones and as the Prosecution rightly invited the jury to conclude, you had one deal left – to be kept for your own use or the remainder of your stock. You had been dealing successfully all day. You have not learnt from past experience. You have not responded to non-custodial or custodial penalties. So the only way society can be protected is imprisonment. Even though it is a term that could be suspended, I will not suspend it because of your history.

In the first case, the defendant DF, who had not offended before, was someone from whom society could be protected by a less harsh sentence than ML. This is likely to be largely attributable to his good character, which as the Judge in the second sentencing remarks points out, ML did not have. ML was therefore not able to claim that the public would be protected from him by virtue of the effects of a non-immediate custodial sentence flowing from this conviction, because previous sentences, including immediate custody, had not protected the public by dissuading him from committing this offence.

In DF, the group to be protected was a large but identifiable demographic – young children who would be abused to produce the photographs of which he had been a consumer. As in legitimate trade, no market survives if its products are not sought out; the market in illegal harmful items, including indecent images, is no different. Meanwhile, in the second case, the group to be protected was not a specific demographic, but geographical and relational groups. The geographical group was the local community who were affected by drug dealing on their doorsteps leading to anti-social behaviour, whilst the relational group included the loved ones of those with drug addictions, whose dependency affected their relationships and families, and also the relatives of those who had been convicted of being involved in the conspiracy.

This sort of societal damage was illustrated with unflinching precision by a Judge sentencing six defendants for a conspiracy to supply Class A drugs:[6]

> Each of you were in an agreement to engage in criminal activity and that activity revolved around possession with intent to supply Class A drugs. Between 25th Oct and 14th Feb each of you played a part in that

6 *R v AC & Ors*, Snaresbrook Crown Court, 2nd September 2019.

possession of Class A drugs and you were participants in the [named] drug line. You, Mr M, have pleaded guilty to a substantive count of being involved in particular supply of the drugs on 14th Nov. As far as the rest of you are concerned, each of you played a role in the possession of Class A drugs with a view to supply.

It is quite obvious that the [road name] area had been blighted for some time with this kind of criminal behaviour: I have heard and read evidence about what was going on in the area. I have seen with my own eyes the video footage – [dealing] taking place in broad daylight in the presence of passers-by; young mothers with children, and there you were brazenly selling drugs to other users. It is a fact that areas such as this are deeply affected by drug dealing. Not only residents, but traders, shopkeepers and others going about their business have to endure this kind of criminal behaviour. [...] it is quite obvious that this was the busiest of lines. It was exceptionally busy as lots of people knew how to contact it to obtain Class A drugs. [...]

Some or all of you will know what I mean when I say that these drugs bring serious harm to those who use them – mentally, physically, countless thousands of people are afflicted by these drugs, and it's not only the individuals who take them who are affected but their families, that they belong to, and society that they are part of, that have to pick up the pieces. Some of you, if not all of you, know what that means as some of you have had this very problem [of addiction]. There is a good reason why these drugs are controlled drugs: they are harmful; they poison people. And what were you doing? You were peddling poison, and that is why the courts take these matters so seriously. Some of you have previous convictions for possessing or supplying drugs. But even if you were not aware of it, it is inconceivable that you would be involved in this sort of operation without realising the consequences if you were caught. Repercussions for your own families, your loved ones, who have to put up with and endure with your behaviour and decision-making processes. I read heartfelt letters from mothers, brothers, sisters, employers; all tell me what a good man you are, and yet there you are peddling poison to others.

In that case, the dealing was taking place in public streets. A more recently recognised phenomenon is 'cuckoo-ing';[7] a drug-dealer befriends a

---

7 Spicer, J., Moyle, L., and Coomber, R. (2019) The variable and evolving nature of 'cuckooing' as a form of criminal exploitation in street level drug markets, *Trends in Organized Crime* (open access), https://link.springer.com/content/pdf/10.1007/s12117-019-09368-5.pdf.

vulnerable, socially isolated person who has their own accommodation, and having gained their trust, uses their address as a base for dealing. The vulnerable resident is usually too frightened to report the matter to the police, or allows the dealers to use their home in return either for drugs, if they are a user, or simply the company of having other people around, which they may be deprived of within the wider community due to their vulnerabilities.

A paradigm example of this is described in the sentencing remarks to SP, a young man who had been convicted by a jury of two counts of possession with intent to supply of Class A drugs, and was sentenced to five years' imprisonment. He had previously been sentenced by the same Judge, at the same court centre, for exactly the same offence four years earlier, when he had received a sentence of 34 months in a Young Offenders' Institution:[8]

> I had hoped that you would have learnt your lesson and that I would never come across you again but unfortunately my hopes of you were misplaced. I have read your letter. You are obviously sincere in what you say, and I fully accept what you say about your mother. But why weren't you thinking about that when you were in the flat at [address] dealing drugs? Why wasn't it as important to you then as it is now? I see sitting behind you your girlfriend of 4 years, who stands by you. Why weren't you thinking of her? It is a very tragic situation I now have to deal with. A young man capable of living an honest life, earning money to look after your girlfriend and your mother, yet you have taken the really easy option. Why bother to get up in the morning and take a job? Why put yourself out when you can sell drugs on the street and make a decent living without having to work? And that's the decision that you took.
>
> And what happened in this case is really, really concerning. Because MW was living at [address] on 4.10.17. He is a man who suffers from paranoid schizophrenia. You were in court when [Z – MW's mental health worker] gave evidence before the jury were sworn at the beginning of this trial. Z and his colleagues from the mental health team had concluded that MW was unfit to give evidence because of his paranoid schizophrenia. He is a 63 year old man living in social housing with the support of the mental health team, on weekly medication by way of injection and oral medication of anti-psychotics. And fortunately for many years he has been relatively stable. But what happened to him was that he came to the attention of people like you. People who knew that he

was a vulnerable, lonely man who would be quite happy to be befriended and then let his premises be used as a base for drug dealing. [...]

There are a number of aggravating factors – the gravest was abuse of vulnerable MW. There are others, such as the fact that you have not learnt your lesson from the earlier sentence. So both counsel are agreed that you fall into Category 3, significant role bracket. Exactly the same Category that you were in when we last met.

When sentencing, the court must consider possible future victims. The imputation in the sentencing remarks of SP is clear – this was the second time that he had been convicted of dealing Class A drugs, and since it had involved a vulnerable member of society, protection was of greater importance than on the previous occasion. That the Judge should refer to SP not having 'learned his lesson' is interesting – but it is unclear whether it is a reference to punishment, rehabilitation, or protection. Considering the lack of hierarchy in s.57(2), the Judge need not make clear to which it referred, and indeed may not even have decided.

In the examples set out above, the sentencing Judges have often identified the need to protect the public from offending as being the justification for an immediate custodial sentence. However, there are cases where the Judge has no choice in the matter – legislation requires them to impose a sentence of at least a specified length due to the nature or frequency of offending. These are often referred to as 'mandatory minimum' sentences, which are returned to below.

Dangerous offenders

Common-sense advocates that offenders from whom it is particularly important that the public are protected are dangerous offenders. The question that automatically follows is 'who is a dangerous offender?' – a question with which the legislature has had to battle, and the answer to which many would say is unsatisfactory.

Much has been written about conceptions of 'dangerousness' – legal, criminological, psychological, neurobiological, and behavioural. This book lacks space to explore this contested and complex concept. However, a little background is necessary to inform our discussion of the role and rationale of 'protection' in sentencing.

The idea of a dangerous offender was not known to English legislation until the Criminal Justice Act 2003. It has been observed that dangerousness itself is a social construct, and it varies with place, time, and societal context.[9] There are also lots of different ways in which offenders may be 'dangerous' – for example, Bottoms and Brownsword criticised the Butler Committee[10] (on 'mentally abnormal offenders') for not including, when it considered dangerous offenders, those who persistently drive dangerously, but were pleased to see that the Floud Report,[11] following a Working Party on the Dangerous Offender established in 1976 by the Howard League for Penal Reform, did tackle this issue.[12]

For these reasons, the use of the label 'dangerous' is not uncontroversial, and neither is the consequence of attaching it to someone. Bennett observes that there are many and varied answers to the question 'what degree of likelihood of future risk should be required before an individual can be said to present a danger of future offending?'[13] Even were that question capable of a clearly defined and satisfactory answer, measuring risk is notoriously difficult, with psychologists disagreeing as to the method by which the most accurate predictions of future risk can be gained.[14] Even the most accurate methods are still far from failsafe.[15]

Nonetheless, criminal justice is an increasingly risk-averse landscape – in 1992 Feeley and Simon identified that 'risk' was emerging as a new, prominent discourse in the United States.[16] Europe has similarly focussed on the notion of risk,[17] and it is perhaps therefore no surprise that the legislature moved to apply this notion within English criminal justice. The perceived advantage of the introduction of the concept of a dangerous offender was that it could be used to garner support for longer sentences for those so identified. Through this route, the populist argument went, the public would

9 European Committee on Crime Problems (2010) The Sentencing, Management and Treatment of Dangerous Offenders, Final Report.
10 Report of the Committee on Mentally Abnormal Offenders (1975) Cmnd. 6244 London: H.M. Stationery Office.
11 Floud, J. and Young, W. (1981) 'Dangerousness and Criminal Justice', London: Heinemann Educational Books.
12 Bottoms, A. E and Brownsword, R. (1982) Dangerousness after the Floud Report, *British Journal of Criminology*, 3(22), pp. 229–254, at p. 230.
13 Bennett, J. (2008) The Social Costs of Dangerousness: Prison and the Dangerous Classes. London: Centre for Crime and Justice Studies, at p. 4.
14 Hilton, N. Z. and Simmons, J. (2001) The Influence of Actuarial Risk Assessment in Clinical Judgements and Tribunal Decisions About Mentally-Disordered Offenders in Maximum Security, *Law and Human Behavior*, 25, pp. 393–408.
15 Moore, R. (2015) A compendium of research and analysis on the Offender Assessment System (OASys) 2009–2013, London: NOMS.
16 Feeley, M. M. and Simon, J. (1992) The New Penology: Notes on the Emerging Strategy of Corrections and Its Implications, *Criminology*, 30(4), pp. 449–474.
17 Beck, U. (2004) 'The Risk Society: Towards a New Modernity'. London: Sage.

be better protected from those who were dangerous to the public due to the nature of their offending. As Lord Dholakia (a Liberal Democrat spokesman on home affairs) observed in the House of Lords when the Bill which became the CJA 03 was being debated, this was not an argument that could be accepted without scrutiny:[18]

> They [articles within the Bill relating to dangerousness] raise an issue of significant public importance. People have strong views about the best way to deal with dangerous offenders. In the course of debate on the amendments, we shall be able to probe the Government's thinking on the subject. We should have an honest debate about sentencing; but equally it is important to identify what works and is good and effective for both defendants and victims.

Introducing dangerousness provisions was clearly going to increase imprisonment – something noted by Lord Carlisle of Bucklow (a Conservative back-bench peer) in the same debate:[19]

> The effect of the clauses taken together is bound to mean a substantial increase in the use of life imprisonment and in sentences of indeterminate length. In themselves, they are bound to increase the prison population. [...] I invite the Minister to tell us what estimate they have of its effect on the prison population, on cost and, as the noble Lord, Lord Thomas, says, on services such as the probation service.

Despite these and various other concerns shared by members of the legislature and many practitioners and other professionals within the criminal justice system,[20] Chapter 5 of the CJA 2003 thus introduced both criteria for determining dangerousness, and the sentencing responses available where it is decided that an offender is dangerous. As noted in Chapter 3 and below, those sentencing options have not been uncontroversial, and have seen changes in the years since the CJA 2003. Nonetheless, the concept of dangerousness remains, and there are sentencing options only available to Judges sentencing dangerous offenders. Consequently, a good place to start

---

18 HL Deb, 14 October 2003, c768.
19 HL Deb, 14 October 2003, c771.
20 E.g. Bennett, J. (2008) The Social Costs of Dangerousness: Prison and the Dangerous Classes. London: Centre for Crime and Justice Studies, at pp. 3–5; and Ashworth, A. and Player, E. (2005) Criminal Justice Act 2003: The Sentencing Provisions, *Modern Law Review*, 68(5), pp. 822–838, at pp. 834–835.

is exploring who is a dangerous offender, according to the Act, before moving to examine how the Act envisages protection being provided.

Who is dangerous?

Section 308 of the Sentencing Act 2020[21] contains the 'assessment of dangerousness'. An offender's 'dangerousness' only falls to be considered if they have been convicted of a specified offence (s.308(1), as defined by s.306). Specified offences are defined by s.306(2): 'specified violent offence' means an offence specified in Part 1 of Schedule 15 to the CJA 03; 'specified sexual offence' means an offence specified in Part 2 of that Schedule; and a 'specified terrorism offence' (added by the Counter-Terrorism and Border Security Act 2019) means an offence specified in Part 3 of that Schedule. This is an immediate challenge to the usefulness of the provision. No matter the apparent motivation or facts of any other offence, if it is not listed within those Parts of the Schedule as a specified violent, sexual, or terrorism offence then an offender who committed it cannot be dangerous as a matter of law, and the sentencing options detailed below are not available. This illustrates the tightly circumscribed and arguably fallacious nature of the assessment of dangerousness.

Where an offender has been convicted for a specified offence, 'it falls to the court to assess whether there is a significant risk to members of the public of serious harm occasioned by the commission by him of further such offences'[22] – this being the 'dangerousness test'. That assessment is undertaken by considering a variety of factors.[23] One of these factors is mandatory,[24] and must be considered, whilst the others are discretionary, and may be considered.

Mandatory status is attached to 'all such information as is available to [the court] about the nature and circumstances of the offence'. Thus the court's focus is clearly aimed at the immediate offence; emphasised by the only discretionary consideration of: the nature and circumstances of any other offences of which the offender has been convicted anywhere in the world;[25] any information available to the court about any pattern of behaviours of

---

21 Formerly s.229 of the CJA 03.
22 S.308(1) SA 20.
23 S.308(2)(a)–(d) of the Sentencing Act 2020.
24 S.308(2)(a).
25 S.308(2)(b).

which this or previous offences form a part;[26] and any information about the offender which is available to the court.[27]

Even where a Judge concludes that an offender is dangerous, they are not required by law to impose a specialised sentence. Therefore, where they consider that the term of custody available to be imposed on the basis of the offence itself will be sufficient without further measures, they may impose a straightforward determinate sentence. An example of this, and also of the use of any other information available to the court as per s.229(2)(c), can be seen in the lengthy sentencing remarks made by the Judge passing sentence on KQ:[28]

> I have to sentence you following a plea of guilty to three counts of possessing a firearm with intent to endanger life. [...].[29] All were loaded. All were found at your home address. Two pistols in a bag in one room, other in another room. All these offences carry a potential life sentence, and the dangerousness provisions apply, and the reason is obvious. Loaded firearms ready and available for use are a very serious matter indeed. When police searched the address you effectively took responsibility, for possession at least, of the firearms. When asked by police whether they were loaded you shrugged. [...]
>
> The issue that has arisen is whether you are in a gang. The prosecution case is you are. [...] I accept that there is no evidence you had an association with gangs over a lengthy period of time and I know not whether, strictly speaking, you are a member of that gang, but it is clear to me that, as you accept in your PSR, at the time of the offences you were associating with serious criminals and gang members; that you were involved with the drugs trade and enforcing that through use of violence. Served only today, and more troubling, is the evidence of firearms themselves. They were all in full working order and loaded with full ammunition. [...]
>
> You were born in [...] 1998 so you are still only 19. You have four previous convictions for six offences, largely drug possession. Also for failure to comply. You have never served a period of detention before. It seems to me your previous convictions mean you cannot be treated as of good character, but they do not aggravate the seriousness of these offences. [...]

---

26 S.308(2)(c).

27 S.308(2)(d).

28 *R v KQ*, Harrow Crown Court, 27th November 2017.

29 The precise type of gun which was the subject of each count has been removed to protect the identity of the defendant.

I've read the pre-sentence report. You told the Probation Officer you had made stupid decisions. Good deal of blame-shifting in your approach. [...]. I acknowledge that your family, here supporting you in force, must be devastated by these events. They must feel that they are about to serve this sentence with you. But the difficulty you face is that you made a choice to associate with people who hold life cheap and who will use violence readily. So you are going to have to take responsibility for consequences of decisions that you have made.

I recognise that you are still very young to be facing a lengthy period of imprisonment, and your letter to me showed that you are an intelligent and articulate young man so you must use your time wisely in prison to gain education and I know your family will play a large role in supporting you.

[Turning to] dangerousness – in the view of a very experienced Probation Officer, you are. In any view in a very short period of time, against a background of no really serious criminal offending, you are in possession with intent of three deadly weapons. On its own that gives me no doubt that you are dangerous, but I don't consider it necessary to pass a dangerousness sentence due to the lengthy sentence you are about to serve. Taking into account, so far as I can, your age and personal mitigation, the sentence, looking at totality, after trial, would have been a sentence of 16 years. Giving credit, the sentence will be 10 years and 8 months concurrent on each count.

As demonstrated here, even in the context of the most serious offending, it is often possible to see the scope for other aims and objectives of sentencing to shine through the cracks. The Judge references a letter written by the defendant, and that it displays a potential for rehabilitation through his imprisonment, supported by his family. Even, and perhaps especially, where an offence is as serious as this one, there is arguably a value to the fact that the sentencing Judge does not have to wrestle with factors that have to be considered hierarchically. This was demonstrated similarly in the case of FN:[30]

Mr N you fall to be sentenced on counts 2 and 3 on this indictment. On 25th January this year, having met V on Grindr, you went to his house for a sexual encounter with him. You strangled him until he became unconscious. After that you assaulted him further – it was gratuitous and inexplicable. You were under the influence of both cannabis and ketamine. After the violence you stole a laptop and other valuable

---

30 *R v FN*, Kingston Crown Court, 4th September 2019.

personal items. You tried to sell that laptop in a shop in Streatham. I have read his VPSs, one dated 25th February, and the latter 19th July. His injuries were nasty – I have looked at photos and can see severe bruising to face. He was unable to see out of one eye for at least a time. He had pain in his mouth for a 2 week period, meaning he couldn't eat properly. His ears and throat were bruised. He associates his flat with the attack and moved as a result. This has affected his work and this has affected him practically in terms of having to get a new passport.[31] This falls into Category 1 – greater harm, as the injuries were serious in the context of the offence and it was a sustained assault in V's own home where he should have felt safe. He thought he was going to be killed that day and one can understand how terrified he must have felt: the offence is aggravated by the location.

The guilty pleas were on the day of trial. V had attended to give evidence. Credit is limited to 10%. You are 27, with one conviction recorded against you that does not aggravate these offences. I have read the PSR and psychiatric report. I take account of the impressive references and of your letter which you have written to me. You are academically able, plainly from a good family. Given your background, although the probation officer notes you may fulfil the dangerousness test in law, I am not satisfied so that I am sure that you do. There is nothing in your history to suggest you would behave this way and no suggestion you would do so again once you have been in prison.

In these final three sentences we see the array of factors influencing the Judge's decision not to find this young man dangerous – familial support, intellect, and her assessment that after prison, he would not behave this way again. Within that is therefore suggested roles for rehabilitation, punishment and deterrence from the three-year custodial sentence passed. Where, however, an offender is found to be dangerous, the sentencing Judge has additional sentencing options available.

Sentencing options for 'dangerous offenders'

With the introduction of the notion of dangerousness in the 2003 Act, there also needed to be sentencing options to respond to that finding; later amendments have left two sentencing options available. IPP, as discussed in Chapter 3, no longer exists.

---

31 One of the 'valuable personal items' stolen, referred to earlier in the remarks, was V's passport.

Life sentence for serious offences[32]

Section 274 SA 20 creates this discretionary life sentence, which requires a finding of dangerousness. It applies only to offences for which the maximum sentence available to the court is life imprisonment.[33] It does not apply to offences of murder, for which the life sentence is mandatory.[34] It is most notable because it does not require any previous convictions. Where the offence carries a maximum of life imprisonment;[35] the court forms the opinion that the offender is dangerous,[36] and the court considers that the seriousness of the offence, alone or in conjunction with others associated with it,[37] justify a life sentence, the imposition of a life sentence becomes mandatory under this provision. As the imposition hinges around the finding of dangerousness and the seriousness of the offence it is hard to argue that there is any focus apart from the protection of the public.

Extended sentence[38]

The extended sentence was brought in by the Legal Aid, Sentencing and Punishment of Offenders Act 2012 to replace IPP. A key failing of IPP was offenders serving much lengthier periods in custody than those intended when the sentence was passed. The legislation introducing extended sentences therefore focussed on the prospect of rehabilitation in the community.

Section 280 sets out the criteria for the imposition of an extended sentence:

- The offender is 21 or over,[39] and convicted of a specified offence[40]
- The court considers that the offender is dangerous[41]
- The court is not required to impose a life sentence[42] and

---

32 S.285 SA 20, formerly in s.225 CJA 03 – for those over 18 but under 21 it is found in s.274.
33 Offences appearing in Schedule 19 to the SA 20 – see s.307.
34 S.275 SA 20.
35 S.285(1)(b).
36 S.285(1)(d).
37 S.285(3).
38 S.279 for those over 21 – s.254 SA 20 for those over 18 but under 21; both formerly within s.226A CJA 03.
39 S.280(1)(b).
40 S.280(1)(a).
41 S.280(1)(c).
42 S.280(1)(d).

either

- The offender had been convicted of an offence listed in Schedule 14 prior to *committing* this offence[43]

or

- The appropriate custodial term under the extended sentence would be at least 4 years[44]

The discretionary nature of the sentence is clear,[45] and where it is imposed, the appropriate custodial term must still be in accordance with s.231(2)[46] – the shortest term commensurate with the seriousness of the offence(s),[47] taking into account the need to impose any mandatory minima.[48]

It is not until s.281(3) that protection as the purpose of such a sentence is mentioned, and it is notable that it is the extension period that is pitched as the part of the sentence that protects the public, as opposed to the appropriate custodial term: 'The extension period must be a period of such length as the court considers necessary for the purpose of protecting members of the public from serious harm occasioned by the commission by the offender of further specified offences'. This length, however, is subject to the requirements specified later in the section, which state that:

- The extension period must be at least 1 year[49]
- The extension period for a specified violent offence cannot be longer than five years[50]
- The extension period for a specified sexual or terrorism offence cannot be longer than eight years[51]
- The total of the appropriate custodial term and the extension period must not be longer than the maximum sentence that was available for the offence when it was committed[52]

It is clear from the use of extended sentences as successors to IPP that there has been a change of position from the legislature – from the idea that

---

43 S.280(3).
44 S.280(4).
45 S.280(1).
46 Formerly s.153(2) CJA 03.
47 S.281(2).
48 S.153(3).
49 S.281(4)(1).
50 S.281(4)(a)(i).
51 S.281(4)(a)(ii).
52 S.281(5).

offenders need to be detained in prison until they are no longer a risk, to the idea that the way to reduce risk is the more careful monitoring of those offenders once they are released back into the community, meaning that they have a greater chance to reintegrate and access rehabilitation.

Mandatory minima[53]

Mandatory minima were first mentioned in Chapter 2 when their prospects for providing deterrence were doubted. They are available in response to a variety of offences and all types of offender – their availability is not restricted to 'dangerous' offenders. Do mandatory minima fare any better as a mechanism for protection than they did for deterrence or rehabilitation? In short, no. They do provide protection to society whilst the defendant is serving the mandatory period. But unless the period of time for which the offender is detained is utilised to enable them to make changes to their thinking processes or to better equip them for a law-abiding life on their release, then a mandated period of imprisonment will be no more effective at protecting the public than a period set by the Judge in accordance with the Sentencing Guidelines.

Even more controversial than mandatory minima, however, was the Imprisonment for Public Protection ('IPP') sentence. Introduced in Chapter 3 dealing with rehabilitation, IPP also warrants consideration in the context of protection.

IPP was itself a mandatory sentence in certain circumstances for a period between IPP's introduction in April 2005,[54] and its being amended in 2008 by s.13(1) of the Criminal Justice and Immigration Act ('CJIA') 2008. The circumstances in which an IPP sentence was mandatory for an offender over 18 in that three-year period were:

- conviction for a 'specified offence' after 4th April 2005, and
- the sentencing court decided that there was a significant risk to members of the public of serious harm being caused by the offender committing further specified offences[55]
- but a sentence of life imprisonment was not available (due to the offence committed) or justified (on the facts of the individual case).

---

53 With thanks to Dominic Lewis for a typically (thought-)provoking conversation on this topic.
54 The date on which IPP as originally enacted in the CJA 03 came into force.
55 For these purposes, 'specified offence' referred to Parts 1 and 2 of Schedule 15 of the 2003 Act, which contained 153 categories of offences.

As the imposition of IPP was mandatory in those circumstances, it caught many offenders who would not otherwise have been subject to such a significant discretionary sentence. The first reported appeal was *Lang*.[56] It focussed on what a sentencing Judge should properly consider before determining that an offender was 'dangerous', and for whom the imposition of an IPP sentence was mandatory. Mr Lang was one of 13 men sentenced to IPP in otherwise unconnected cases who appealed against the imposition of that sentence. It is noteworthy, such that it appears in the opening paragraph of the judgment, that 'in none [of the cases] was the specified period to be served under section 82A of the Powers of Criminal Court (Sentencing) Act 2000,[57] greater than three-and-a-half years and in three it was 18 months or less'. Therefore, the longest tariff period that had been given to any of the appellants was the equivalent of a seven-year determinate prison sentence (giving a specified period of three-and-a-half years).

In July 2008, the CJIA 2008 amended the criteria for IPP, and made it effectively discretionary, even where an offender had been found to be dangerous under the CJA 2003. The new criterion was that before an IPP sentence could be passed, the offender had to fulfil one of two conditions:[58]

• At the time the offence was committed, the offender had been convicted of an offence specified in Schedule 15A,[59] or,
• The notional minimum term[60] is at least two years[61]

This would have the effect of narrowing eligibility for IPP to those who had committed more serious offences than those for which it had originally been available. In relation to the first condition, Sch.15A contains fewer offences than the list of 'specified offences' in Sch.15.[62] It is very similar to

---

56 [2005] EWCA Crim 286.
57 This is the tariff period – the length of imprisonment that would have been imposed as a determinate sentence having regard to the seriousness of harm and level of culpability of the offence, and taking into account the early release provisions. Section 82A is now s.323 SA 20.
58 Ss.(3A) and (3B).
59 Ss.(3A).
60 The period required for punishment for the offence – representing the determinate sentence that the offender would have received had they not been given an IPP sentence.
61 Ss.(3B).
62 As explained by the Court of Appeal in *Lang*, at [6]; 'A specified offence may or may not be serious (section 224). It will be serious if it is punishable, in the case of a person aged 18 or over, with 10 years' imprisonment or more (section 224(2)(b)). If serious, it through s.225 CJA 03 may attract life imprisonment or imprisonment for public protection for an adult (section 225) or detention for life or detention for public protection for those under 18 on the day of conviction (section 225). It will attract such a sentence if the court is of opinion that there is a significant risk to members of the public of serious harm by the commission of further specified offences (section 225(1) and section 226(1))'.

the list of 'serious offences' found in s.109 of the Powers of Criminal Courts (Sentencing) Act 2000, as amended by the Sexual Offences Act 2003, with some further offences from the Sexual Offences Act 2003, and a catch-all provision for attempted offences under the Criminal Attempts Act 1981.

The second condition, that the offender would receive a notional minimum term of at least two years, means that (due to s.82A of the Powers of Criminal Courts (Sentencing) Act 2000 and s.28 of the Crime (Sentences) Act 1997), an offender would have to be facing a determinate sentence of at least four years' imprisonment before the sentencing Judge could consider imposing an IPP sentence.

If either of those conditions was satisfied, the next question was whether there was a significant risk of serious harm. If there was, then there still remained two further requirements of which the court had to be satisfied before it imposed an IPP sentence. First, was it necessary to impose a special form of sentence (i.e. something other than a determinate sentence) at all? Secondly, if it was necessary, then was an IPP or an extended sentence[63] the appropriate option?

As detailed in Chapter 3, not only did many offenders receive IPP, but many are still serving. Whilst protection for the public during the period of incarceration is assured, the cost to offenders of the method is troubling.

Life sentence tariffs and the whole life order

Any offender who receives a life sentence, whether mandatory for murder, or discretionary for any other offence which carries a maximum of life imprisonment, has a tariff period set by the trial Judge. This is the minimum length of imprisonment that they must serve before they are able to apply to the Parole Board for release. In the past, the period that someone who was sentenced to life would serve was decided by the Home Secretary, who had the power to order the release of life sentence prisoners on review.[64] This meant that such a prisoner did not know how long they would have to serve at the time that the sentence was handed down, as the Home Secretary

---

63 This refers to extended sentences under s.227 CJA 03, which must not be confused with the current 'extended determinate sentence' that replaced IPP on its repeal, and which are discussed earlier in this chapter.

64 Section 61(1) of the Criminal Justice Act 1967 conferred a discretion on the Home Secretary to release on licence a prisoner serving a life sentence if recommended to do so by the Parole Board, which was created by the same Act. This power was subsequently again conferred on the Home Secretary by section 35(2) and (3) of the Criminal Justice Act 1991, and later (in terms substantially identical to those of the 1991 Act) in section 29 of the Crime (Sentences) Act 1997.

would only act on recommendations from the Parole Board once they had reviewed the prisoner's application for release. However, this practice was ruled by the House of Lords to offend against the separation of powers,[65] and the setting of a tariff period is now undertaken by the sentencing Judge in all cases, and in accordance with Schedule 21 of the CJA 2003 in murder cases.

Capital punishment

It is notable that a whole life order is the most severe sentence known to the English system. Capital punishment's final vestige in this country was the death penalty for murder. This was abolished in 1969. In the years before its abolition, the use of capital punishment had been much reduced by the Homicide Act 1957, which removed the automaticity of the death penalty for any murder, though exceptions were maintained, including any murder committed for the purpose of stealing items from the deceased. Indeed, the final two people to be hanged in England received the death penalty for just such a murder – Gwynne Evans and Peter Allen had bludgeoned a man to death to steal the princely sum of £10, and were hanged for that offence on 13th August 1964.[66]

On 28th October 1965, a Private Member's Bill to suspend the death penalty, sponsored by the MP Sydney Silverman, received Royal Assent. On 9th November 1965, the Murder (Abolition of Death Penalty) Act 1965 suspended the death penalty for murder in the United Kingdom for a period of five years. In December 1969, the House of Commons reaffirmed its decision that capital punishment for murder should be permanently abolished. On a free vote, the House voted by 343 to 185, a majority of 158, that the Murder (Abolition of Death Penalty) Act 1965, should not expire. Thus, the death penalty for murder was formally abolished.

Examples of other jurisdictions' approaches

The American approach

Whilst the death penalty can be seen as the ultimate in punishment and protection, it inevitably excludes any other aim of sentencing, and carries with it a terrible history of miscarriages of justice which can never be righted. Nonetheless, its use persists in many of the states of the United States. In

---

65 *R v Secretary of State for the Home Department, ex parte Anderson* [2002] UKHL 46.
66 www.theguardian.com/world/2014/aug/13/britain-last-executions-hanging-criminals-low -key [accessed 9th October 2020].

2020, 30 of the 50 states still retained the death penalty.[67] The frequency of its usage and its most recent usage, however, vary drastically between states. Whilst in Kansas the death penalty remains on the statute books, no one has been executed for a crime since 1965. However, in 2020, there were 17 executions across the United States.[68] Whilst ten of these were federal, the other seven were state-ordered. These were ordered by, and carried out in, Texas (three), Alabama (one), Tennessee (one), Georgia (one), and Missouri (one).[69]

The relative prevalence of the use of the death penalty can be seen alongside the greater use of prescriptive and constrictive sentencing matrices in the United States – though a variety of guideline structures, with variation in the possibility of departing from them or accessing appellate review of them, exist across the states. In many states this is in contrast to the guideline system seen in England, with scope for departing where that can be justified by unusual circumstances, and the possibility of appeals on the basis of either error of law, or a manifestly excessive sentence, where the Sentencing Guidelines are not applied (or departed from) appropriately.

Take as an example Tennessee. Tennessee has already stayed three executions scheduled for mid-2020 due to the coronavirus pandemic,[70] and there was a further man due to be executed on 3rd December 2020,[71] however a temporary reprieve was granted.[72] There have been 13 executions in Tennessee since 2000.[73] Tennessee uses a sentencing grid, and legislation provides that the length of the prison sentence found in each matrix cell is mandatory – the court may not sentence outside of the range even if aggravating or mitigating offence facts are present.[74] This is despite the Tennessee

67 https://worldpopulationreview.com/state-rankings/death-penalty-states [accessed 9th October 2020].
68 https://deathpenaltyinfo.org/executions/2020 [accessed 20th December 2020].
69 A number of further executions, both state-ordered and federal were delayed to 2021 due to the coronavirus pandemic.
70 Oscar Smith (June) – https://eu.tennessean.com/story/news/2020/04/17/coronavirus-tennessee-court-delays-execution-citing-covid-19/5138614002/; Byron Black (August) https://eu.tennessean.com/story/news/crime/2020/06/12/second-tennessee-execution-delayed-2021-over-covid-19-concerns/3178956001/; and Harold Nichols (August) https://eu.tennessean.com/story/news/crime/2020/07/17/harold-wayne-nichols-execution-august-tennessee-bill-lee-covid-19/5461947002/ [accessed 9th October 2020].
71 www.themarshallproject.org/next-to-die/tn [accessed 9th October 2020].
72 https://innocenceproject.org/pervis-payne-wrongful-conviction-what-to-know-innocent-tennessee/ [accessed 2nd December 2020].
73 www.tn.gov/correction/statistics-and-information/executions/tennessee-executions.html [accessed 15th October 2020].
74 Tenn. Code Ann. § 40-35-210(c).

guidelines being technically advisory,[75] and indeed this combination is identified by the Sentencing Guidelines Resource Center at the Robina Institute of Criminal Law and Criminal Justice as being an unusual feature.[76]

The Norwegian approach

The American position can be starkly contrasted with that seen in Nordic countries, where even mass murders do not tend to lead to a life sentence. For example, Anders Breivik was convicted of the murder of 77 people: on 22nd July 2011, he killed eight people by detonating a bomb in a van in Oslo, then shot dead 69 participants at a Workers' Youth League (AUF) summer camp on the island of Utøya.[77] For these offences, he was convicted and sentenced to 21 years' 'preventive detention'; the maximum sentence available to the court under Norwegian law (with the exception of genocide and war crimes, for which 30 years is available[78]).[79] In their sentencing comments, Judge Arne Lyng expressed some reservations about the sufficiency of this term for the purposes of protection: 'It is hard to imagine', the judgment continues, 'that such a term-limited sentence is sufficient to protect this country from this man'.

In Norway, 'preventive detention' is, theoretically, an indeterminate sentence.[80] However, a period, akin to a tariff period in England and Wales, has to be set and this cannot be more than 21 years.[81] It is generally not more than 15 years. Offenders rarely serve more than 14 years, though it is of course possible that someone could be detained indefinitely. To give some context, the average custodial sentence length across all custodial sentences in 2020 in Norway is 10.7 months.[82] Meanwhile, in England and Wales, the

---

75 https://sentencing.umn.edu/profiles/tennessee/ [accessed 9th October 2020].
76 https://sentencing.umn.edu/profiles/tennessee/ under heading 'What Makes Tennessee Unique?' [accessed 9th October 2020].
77 www.bbc.co.uk/news/world-europe-14259989 [accessed 9th October 2020].
78 www.theatlantic.com/international/archive/2012/08/a-different-justice-why-anders-breivik-only-got-21-years-for-killing-77-people/261532/ [accessed 12th October 2020].
79 www.nytimes.com/2012/08/25/world/europe/anders-behring-breivik-murder-trial.html [accessed 9th October 2020].
80 www.prison-insider.com/countryprofile/prisons-norway2019 [accessed 12th October 2020].
81 http://www.ilafengsel.no/preventive_detension.html [accessed 12th October 2020].
82 https://journals.sagepub.com/doi/abs/10.1177/0032885505276969.

average custodial sentence length is 19.6 months – the highest in a decade, and nearly twice that of Norway.[83]

Whilst this is a very small snapshot of only two other jurisdictions, necessarily constrained by space, it serves to illustrate that protection can be provided in a variety of ways, and how it is conceived in different jurisdictions varies. Whilst the death penalty from the United States' perspective, and shorter prison sentences from Norway's perspective, can both be said to provide protection, they are not directed only at that imperative. The death penalty can be viewed as a punishment, whilst the Norwegian approach is strong in its belief in rehabilitation of even those offenders who have committed mass murders.

Conclusion

Protection of the public will always be an inescapable aspect of criminal justice – crime causes distress, physical harm, loss of property, and costs taxpayers large sums, as money is needed by the state to fund police forces, criminal courts, prisons, and support services for those affected by crime. How that protection is conferred varies across the world, from the Nordic penal exceptionalism, through to the continuing availability in 28 American states (plus the Federal Government and the military) of the death penalty,[84] though some states have not put anyone to death for many years.[85] England remains in the middle, maintaining the mandatory life sentence for murder, and discretionary life sentences for other offences, but only imposing a 'whole life order' in the most egregious cases of murder, such as multiple murders and those motivated by terrorist ideologies.

---

83 April 2019–March 2020 https://assets.publishing.service.gov.uk/government/uploads/system/uploads/attachment_data/file/910530/criminal-justice-statistics-quarterly-march-2020.pdf [accessed 12th October 2020].
84 https://files.deathpenaltyinfo.org/documents/pdf/FactSheet.f1605882308.pdf [accessed 2nd December 2020].
85 E.g. Kansas, who last executed a prisoner in 1965 – see www.pewresearch.org/fact-tank/2019/03/14/11-states-that-have-the-death-penalty-havent-used-it-in-more-than-a-decade/ [accessed 2nd December 2020].

5   Sentencing as reparation

Reparation: The action of making amends for a wrong one has done, by providing payment or other assistance to those who have been wronged.
(Oxford English Dictionary)

The concept of reparation is woven throughout the sentencing process. It is seen most commonly in ancillary orders, such as the provision of monetary compensation or forfeiture of physical items. However it can also feature through restitution orders, the victim surcharge, and the award of costs. Considering reparation in a completely different way, the medium of restorative justice offers the opportunity in certain appropriate cases for an offender to meet with the victims of the offence that they committed, in an effort to aid dialogue and mutual understanding – of the consequences for the victim, and how the offender came to commit the offence.

Some would argue that one of the weaknesses in English law and procedure is that restorative justice techniques are not available as a diversionary tactic for adult offenders, but rely on there being a conviction before it can be undertaken. That it only becomes an option once someone has pleaded guilty[1] means that whilst it may reduce the likelihood of the commission of a further offence, it has not had the opportunity to do so without the defendant being convicted of the first offence, which will then stay on their record. For first time offenders, this could be seen as an opportunity for

1 The legislation only permits deferment for a restorative justice activity after a conviction. However, it is explicitly stated in the Ministry of Justice Pre-sentence restorative justice (RJ) guidance that deferral of sentence for an RJ activity is only suitable where that conviction results from a guilty plea, as opposed to conviction after a contested trial – Ministry of Justice (2014) *Pre-sentence restorative justice (RJ)*, London: Ministry of Justice, at p. 7. This is coherent, as if an offender does not accept that they committed the crime then there could be nothing to be gained by discussion of it with the person who claims that they did.

DOI: 10.4324/9781003201625-5

true diversion, leading to a reduction in crime, de facto rehabilitation, and consequent protection of the public, that the system is currently missing out on, perhaps as part of the legislature's misguided quest for 'maximum punishment' (see Chapters 1 and 2). Undoubtedly the current system focuses on reparation as the return of goods or the quantification of harms such that monetary compensation can be paid. This narrow scope of reparation, as well as its inclusion only at the sentencing stage, is an area on which reform could usefully be focussed.

Compensation

In many criminal cases, the most obvious form of reparation that is offered is by way of compensation payable directly to the victim. The possibility of including compensation as part of sentencing has been around for many years – in 1982, Parliament introduced a compensation order as a sentencing option in its own right.[2] Currently, the legislation governing the ordering of compensation is sections 133–146 of the Sentencing Act 2020.

Ashworth characterises compensation as the retrospective cousin of punishment – one is forward-looking whilst the other is concerned with righting a wrong in the past.[3] Whilst some regard compensation as the natural result of criminal activities to be ordered alongside a punishment,[4] others argue that the provision of compensation as a sentence should be sufficient alone.[5]

Whilst damage to replaceable property (though not that of sentimental value) can often be easily quantified by the value of the item or the cost of repairs, not all damage that may be caused as a result of crime has an easily identified financial value. For example, monetary compensation may be ordered in a case where someone has suffered physical harm or psychological distress. In such cases, compensation may be ordered due to the cost of particular treatment that is not covered entirely by the National Health Service (e.g. complex dental treatment required as a result of a blow to the mouth). However, it may also be ordered in relation to the physical injury suffered, something which has no directly quantifiable financial value.

To assist a court in quantifying the 'value' of an injury, the Sentencing Council has developed a guide which is based upon the tariff amounts used

---

2 Section 67 of the Criminal Justice Act 1982.
3 Ashworth, A. (1986) Punishment and Compensation: Victims, Offenders and the State, *Oxford Journal of Legal Studies*, 6(1), 86–122, at p. 92.
4 Schafer, S. (1970) 'Compensation and Restitution to Victims of Crime' (2nd edn), part IV.
5 Barnett, R. E. (1977) Restitution: a New Paradigm of Criminal Justice, *Ethics*, 87, p. 279.

by the Criminal Injuries Compensation Authority.[6] For example, in the realm of physical injuries, a black eye has a suggested starting point of £125, whilst the loss of a front tooth has a starting point of £1,500 per tooth. Meanwhile, 'disabling mental anxiety, lasting more than six weeks, medically verified', where mental injury is properly described as 'disabling' if it has 'a substantial adverse effect on a person's ability to carry out normal day-to-day activities for the time specified (e.g. impaired work or school performance or effects on social relationships or sexual dysfunction)', has a starting point of £1,000. Where a person has experienced sexual abuse, the degree of that abuse influences the starting point for compensation, with non-penetrative sexual acts performed over clothing having a suggested starting point of £1,000. These figures are applicable in the Magistrates' Court (there is no such guidance for the Crown Court), and as the Sentencing Council guidance notes, it would be rare for such offences to be dealt with in the Magistrates' Court.[7] However, sexual assaults involving adult defendants and complainants, where there is touching over clothing, are sometimes tried in the Magistrates' Court, reflecting an increased emphasis on the Magistrates' Court retaining jurisdiction wherever possible,[8] relieving pressure on the Crown Courts.[9]

The importance of compensation within the criminal justice system is reinforced by the fact that consideration of awarding it is mandatory: the court *can* make a compensation order in any case where the offender has caused loss to another through the offence.[10] It can either be an ancillary order, or a sentence in its own right.[11] The court must give reasons if it decides not to order compensation.[12] Although there is no limit to the amount of compensation that an offender aged 18 or over can be ordered to pay,[13]

---

6 www.sentencingcouncil.org.uk/explanatory-material/magistrates-court/item/fines-and-fi nancial-orders/compensation/2-suggested-starting-points-for-physical-and-mental-injuries/ [accessed 23rd May 2021].

7 *Ibid*, at the bottom of the web page.

8 See the Sentencing Council's Allocation Guideline: www.sentencingcouncil.org.uk/wp-con tent/uploads/Allocation-definitive-guideline-Web.pdf [accessed 24th September 2020].

9 And as noted in the SC's assessment of the Allocation Guideline, it did indeed result in a smaller proportion of adult defendants being sent to the Crown Court for trial, though it also resulted in an increase in defendants being proceeded against in the Magistrates' Court and then being committed for sentence to the Crown Court: www.sentencingcouncil.org.uk /wp-content/uploads/Allocation-assessment.pdf [accessed 24th September 2020].

10 S.133 of the SA 20, formerly s.130(2A) Powers of Criminal Courts (Sentencing) Act 2000.

11 S.134(2) SA 20.

12 S.55 of the Sentencing Act 2020, formerly s.130(3) PCC(S)A 2000.

13 The Crown Court has always had unlimited powers to fine. Prior to 2013, the Magistrates' Courts Act (MCA) 1980, s.40(1) limited the maximum amount of compensation that a

the amount must be set by reference to their means.[14] This is consistent with reparation within the wider context of the other aims and objectives set by s.57 – if an offender is required to pay an amount that is outside of their means, then it creates a risk that they will commit further criminal offences to obtain it, thus compromising rehabilitation and deterrence within their sentence. It has been made clear by the appellate courts that compensation should only be ordered where it is 'realistic' that the offender will have the means to pay the sum, and within a reasonable amount of time.[15]

Whilst a fine is a sum of money ordered to be paid for punitive reasons, compensation is not meant to punish the offender (though it will sometimes have that effect); it is designed to give some reparation to the victim. This is why defendants sometimes receive a sentence comprising of both a fine and compensation.[16] This difference is underscored by the fact that a fine is payable to the state, and not the victim, and that compensation is given priority over a fine where the offender will not have the means to pay both.[17]

Sometimes, where a defendant is of limited means, the court may prioritise compensation over the imposition of a fine. For example, when sentencing YM for two offences – one of common assault by beating of a shop worker and another of obstructing a police officer – the magistrates decided to impose a fine as regards the obstruction, but compensation instead of a fine as regards the shopworker:[18]

> Regarding the assault we're going to award compensation to Mr L of £160 instead of a fine. Regarding costs for trial, we make order for £150 of costs bearing in mind that you are on Disability Living Allowance. Also for the obstruction we give you an £80 fine, on the basis of your credit for guilty plea. You will pay a victim surcharge of £20.

In addition to the general power to award compensation, there are also statutory footings for the award of compensation in particular defined

---

Magistrates' Court could order to £5,000 per charge. However, Sch.16, para 8(1) to the Crime and Courts Act 2013 amended PCC(S)A 00, s.131 to remove this limit. A table of the relevant limits by date of offence are found in s.142(4)(b) of the SA 20.

14 S.135(3), formerly s.130(11) PCC(S)A 00. This is consistent with the position on fines, which must also be set with reference to the offender's means under s.124(1) SA 20 (formerly s.164 Criminal Justice Act 2003), and with reference to the Sentencing Guideline on Over-arching Principles.

15 *Inwood* (1974) 60 Cr App R 70, at p. 72.

16 See, for example, the case of YM, below.

17 Formerly section 130(12) PCC(S)A 00, now s.135(4) SA 20.

18 *R v YM*, Aylesbury Magistrates' Court, 13th May 2016.

circumstances. Whilst these will not be addressed in detail, they again underscore the importance of compensation through the breadth of its availability. First, s.137(1) and (2) SA 20[19] permit compensation where property has been removed from its owner via an offence under the Theft Act 1968 or the Fraud Act 2006, and whilst it is out of the lawful owner's possession, suffers damage in any way, but is then recovered and returned to the lawful owner. Secondly, s.136(2) SA 20[20] sets out that a compensation order may only be made as a result of an accident arising from the presence of a motor vehicle on a road if either s.130(5) applies, or the compensation is awarded in respect of injury, loss, or damage due to an accident arising from the presence of a motor vehicle on the road if the offender was uninsured in respect of that damage, and compensation is not payable by the Motor Insurer's Bureau.[21]

Restitution Orders

Whilst compensation orders (with the exception of those made under s.137) tend to be made on the basis of either personal injury, or that a tangible item was taken and not returned, restitution orders address the situation where the offender has retained the property that is the subject of the charge.

Section 148 of the Sentencing Act 2020[22] provides that a restitution order can be made by a court where goods[23] have been stolen, and the offender is convicted of either any offence with reference to the theft (whether or not the stealing is the main gravamen of the offence), or any other offence where an offence referable to the theft is being taken into consideration[24] at sentencing. There are various ways in which the court can give effect to a restitution order, depending upon whether the offender still has the goods in their possession, or whether they have passed them on to another or used them as security for a loan.[25]

---

19 Formerly s.130(5) PCC(S)A 00.
20 Formerly s.130(6) PCC(S)A 00.
21 S.136(3) SA 20.
22 Formerly s.148 PCC(S)A 00.
23 As defined by s.151(4) SA 20, formerly s.148(10) PCC(S)A 00; '"goods", except so far as the context otherwise requires, includes money and every other description of property (within the meaning of the Theft Act 1968) except land, and includes things severed from the land by stealing'.
24 This means that the offender has admitted to the offence, with which he has not been charged, and so no separate charges will be brought in relation to it, but it will be considered when passing sentence.
25 See sections 147–149 SA 20, formerly s.148 and 149 PCC(S)A 00.

This power is relatively little used – in the calendar year 2019 there were 47 such orders made in England and Wales.[26] 31 of these were made in Crown Courts, including one case where two orders were made on different days. In Magistrates' Courts there were 16 Restitution Orders made in 2019. The Court of Appeal has encouraged sentencing courts to be mindful of this power and to make use of it.[27]

Short of being ordered by the court to restore items to a victim of crime through a Restitution Order, however, it is often within the power of the offender to organise the payment of a sum that they claimed dishonestly, if this came through a Government department – such as the overclaiming of benefits.[28] For example, NM had claimed Jobseekers' Allowance when she had not declared the true extent of her savings. She was charged with, and pleaded guilty to, one charge contrary to s.111A(1)(a) of the Social Security Administration Act 1992 – dishonestly making a false representation with a view to obtaining a benefit. The bench that sentenced her indicated their surprise that she had not sought to repay the amounts she had received to which she had not been entitled, which amounted to nearly £5,500 claimed over three years between 2011 and 2014:

> This offence is serious enough for us to make a Community Order. This will last for 12 months and you will have to complete 120 hours' unpaid work. We have taken into account your early guilty plea albeit at a later stage and there's a small reduction for that. In 2011 there was no victim surcharge for Community Orders so there is none for this offence. We have listened on costs and order that you pay £320. We are surprised you have made no attempt to pay any of the money back and we feel that you could have paid any amount to show willingness to do so prior to the case coming to court.

In addition to repayment of money wrongly obtained, or the payment to represent loss occasioned by the offence itself, offenders are often required to pay sums of money in costs and a victim surcharge.

Running the criminal justice system is not a cheap undertaking: figures from the Institute for Government, part of the Chartered Institute of Public Finance and Accountancy, show that in the financial year 2018/2019, Her

---

26 These figures were obtained through a Freedom of Information request to the Ministry of Justice – number 200924001.

27 *Webbe* [2001] EWCA Crim 1217, at [32].

28 www.gov.uk/benefit-overpayments/how-to-make-a-repayment [accessed 23rd November 2020].

Majesty's Courts and Tribunals Service had an operational spend of £2 billion.[29] This is despite that cost representing a reduction of 18.4% in real terms since 2010/2011.[30] Therefore, it is important that the criminal justice system attempts to recoup even small amounts of its running costs.

Whilst the concept of requiring offenders to make at least some contribution towards the costs incurred by the state providing the staff and buildings in which criminal proceedings take place is nothing new, there have been more recent mechanisms introduced to try to increase the contribution of offenders to services that are required as a result of criminal behaviour. A not uncontroversial example of this is the victim surcharge.

Victim surcharge

In this way, there is also wider reparation built into every single sentence passed by the victim surcharge, found in s.42 SA 20. That section requires a court, when dealing with an offender for one or more offences, to order the offender to pay a surcharge. The amount of surcharge will vary depending on the type of sentence imposed[31] and whether the defendant was under 18 on the offence date. If sentenced to custody, the Crown Court cannot permit the surcharge to be 'served' as additional time in custody,[32] illustrating the importance attached by the legislature to provide some financial recompense by those convicted of any offence, which cannot be 'substituted' for extra time being served.

The victim surcharge has to be imposed whenever an offender is sentenced, and cannot be waived. By virtue of s.42(3) of the SA 20,[33] where the court considers that it would be appropriate to make a compensation order[34] but the offender has insufficient means to pay both the surcharge and the appropriate compensation order,[35] the court must reduce the surcharge accordingly, if necessary to nil. It will be expected that if this is done the only justification was that the offender had insufficient means to pay both.[36]

---

29 www.instituteforgovernment.org.uk/publication/performance-tracker-2019/criminal-courts [accessed 23rd November 2020].

30 *Ibid.*

31 The more severe the sentence, the greater the amount of the surcharge.

32 CPS Sentencing Overview www.cps.gov.uk/legal-guidance/sentencing-overview#:~:text=Guidance%20under%20Costs.-,Victims%20Surcharge,person%20to%20pay%20a%20surcharge.&text=If%20sentenced%20to%20custody%2C%20the,as%20additional%20time%20in%20custody [accessed 25th September 2020].

33 Formerly s.161A(3) CJA 03.

34 S.161A(3)(a) – or a slavery and trafficking reparation order or an unlawful profit order.

35 S.161A(3)(b).

36 *Hare and Purse* [2016] EWCA Crim 1355, at [18]–[19].

An example of the interplay between costs (see below), compensation (see above), and the victim surcharge was seen in the case of CC.[37] CC had pleaded guilty to an offence of racially aggravated harassment in somewhat unusual circumstances. Having been taken to Accident and Emergency suffering from an epileptic fit (though conscious and responsive), she had racially abused a nurse who was treating her, whom CC thought was conversing with another nurse in a language that was not English.

When sentencing CC the Bench performed the following calculation:

> Taking all that [the facts of the offence and the mitigation] into account we impose a fine of £160. We halve the legal costs to £40. But we are going to award compensation to someone who faced that verbal attack so that's £50. No victim surcharge so a total of £250.

The victim surcharge was originally introduced as a flat rate of £15, and imposed only when the offender was sentenced by way of a fine.[38] Over time it has been expanded to apply to all sentence disposals, including conditional discharges.[39] The amount is decided by reference to the date on which the offence was committed, not the date on which sentence was passed.[40] Currently the amount is decided by reference to the nature and length of the sentence passed – the existing figures represent a rise of 5% from the previous amounts applicable to offences committed before 14th April 2020.[41]

Income from the victim surcharge contributes to the Ministry of Justice's Victim and Witness Fund.[42] That Fund issues grants to the geographical Police and Crime Commissioners across the country, who in turn commission local support services for victims in their communities. It also funds nationally commissioned support such as: 94 rape support centres across England and Wales, the court-based Witness Service, and the National Homicide Service.[43] Examples of some of the organisations which benefit-

---

37 *R v CC*, Uxbridge Magistrates' Court, 3rd October 2016.
38 The victim surcharge was first introduced by s.161A of the Criminal Justice Act 2003, which was inserted by s.14 of the Domestic Violence, Crime and Victims Act 2004. It applied to all offences committed after 1st April 2007. Initially it amounted to £15 but was only imposed if a fine formed part of the sentence, per the Criminal Justice Act 2003 (Surcharge) (No 2) Order 2007, SI 2007/1079.
39 Though it does not apply where someone is given an absolute discharge – s.42(5)(a).
40 www.sentencingcouncil.org.uk/about-sentencing/types-of-sentence/other-orders-made -on-sentencing/what-is-the-victim-surcharge/ [accessed 18th November 2020].
41 The Criminal Justice Act 2003 (Surcharge) (Amendment) Order 2020.
42 www.sentencingcouncil.org.uk/about-sentencing/types-of-sentence/other-orders-made -on-sentencing/what-is-the-victim-surcharge/ [accessed 18th November 2020].
43 www.gov.uk/guidance/victim-and-witness-funding-awards [accessed 25th September 2020].

ted from the Victim and Witness Fund in 2018 and 2019 (the most recent data available) can be seen on the Ministry of Justice website.[44] This demonstrates the importance attached by the legislature to those who are prosecuted by the criminal justice system having to 'pay back' into the system to help support the costs of providing services that are needed by victims of crime.

Criticism has been directed at the victim surcharge – chiefly that Judges have no discretion as to whether to impose it, regardless of the offender's means, and that it is not related to, or adjusted to reflect, the type of offence committed, including level of harm caused or the loss suffered by the victim. Writing in 2013, Joshua Rozenberg noted that raising the amount of the surcharge, and applying it to all other disposal types as well as fines was,[45] 'an irresistible opportunity to look tough and raise cash for services that, if really needed, should be state-funded'. Furthermore, the extension of the surcharge to apply to all offences, regardless of the type of disposal, and with no judicial discretion, meant that offenders with absolutely no means still had to have it imposed upon them.[46] Similarly, those who were mentally ill, other than those subject to a Mental Health Act disposal such as a hospital order,[47] would still have to pay, as would those sentenced to life imprisonment.

Judicial innovations can lessen the impact of the requirement to pay the victim surcharge, as in this example when sentencing MB to six months' imprisonment suspended for two years with a requirement of 30 Rehabilitation Activity Requirement days for possession of an offensive weapon:[48]

> The victim surcharge must also be added and you can pay that at rate of £5 per week; first payment a week on Friday.

However, for offenders who are completely impecunious, even sensible thinking of that kind will not solve the problem. Erin Sanders-McDonagh, arguing for the abolition of the victim surcharge, noted that, for those offenders without the means to pay, the victim surcharge can 'result in a spiral of

---

44 *Ibid.*
45 www.lawgazette.co.uk/law/victim-surcharge-unintended-consequences-/71546.article [accessed 23rd May 2021].
46 Creating a Gordian knot – it was permissible to reduce the surcharge down to nil if there was compensation ordered to be paid and D could not pay both the compensation and the surcharge, but where compensation cannot be ordered as D has no means, the surcharge must still be imposed.
47 No surcharge is payable where such a disposal is used – s.42(5)(b).
48 *R v MB*, St Albans Crown Court, 12th February 2018.

debt they cannot pay – and in many cases effectively become imprisoned for poverty.'[49] Clearly in those circumstances the wider aims of s.57 are fatally undermined – failure to comply with an administrative charge aimed at reparation leads to wholly disproportionate punishment, without any realistic hope of deterrence (as the offender did not and will not have the means to pay), no rehabilitation, and in circumstances where there is no need to protect the public.

Costs

It is common for a convicted defendant to be ordered to pay some of the costs of their prosecution.[50] Again, this can be seen as having a wider reparative imperative. The criminal justice system is expensive to run, and the large majority of prosecutions are funded by the state.[51]

The Court of Appeal has issued guidance on the making of costs orders,[52] which help to locate the role of costs within the sentencing process, and also to examine how they fit in with the aims and objectives in s.57(2) SA 20:[53]

- an order for costs should never exceed the sum which, having regard to the offender's means and any other financial order imposed, they are able to pay, and which it is reasonable to order them to pay;[54]
- an order for costs should never exceed the sum which the prosecutor actually and reasonably incurred;
- the purpose of the order is to compensate the prosecutor. Thus if conduct of the defence has caused the prosecutor avoidable expense, the offender may be ordered to pay some or all of those expenses. However, the offender must not be punished for pleading not guilty and defending themselves, and neither should they be punished if the trial took longer than it should have done due to counsel taking unnecessary points;[55]

49 www.kent.ac.uk/news/society/25032/expert-comment-victim-surcharge-fee-should-be-dissolved [accessed 25th September 2020].

50 S.18(1)(a) Prosecution of Offences Act 1985. There are other circumstances in which costs orders can be made against defendants, e.g. if they lose on appeal, but these are not covered in this book.

51 Private prosecutions, permitted under s.6(1) of the Prosecution of Offences Act 1985, make up a much smaller proportion of the annual figures.

52 *Northallerton Magistrates' Court, ex p Dove* [2000] 1 Cr App R (S) 136, at p. 137.

53 List adapted from Freer, E. (2019) 'A Practitioners' Guide to Ancillary Orders in Criminal Courts', London: Bloomsbury Professional.

54 Confirming *R v Nottingham Justices, ex p Fohmann* [1987] 84 Cr App R 316, at p. 319.

55 *Jones v Guildford Crown Court* [2004] EWHC 2939 (Admin), at [12].

- the costs ordered to be paid should not be grossly disproportionate to any fine imposed for the offence.[56] Whilst not an arithmetical relationship, costs should be viewed in the context of the maximum penalty considered by Parliament to be appropriate for the offence;
- if the total of the proposed fine and the costs sought by the prosecutor exceeds the sum which the offender could reasonably be ordered to pay, the costs order should be reduced rather than the fine;
- it is for the offender to provide details of their means so the court can come to an affordable penalty. If such details are not provided then the court can draw reasonable inferences from its knowledge of the case.
- if the court proposes to make any financial order against the offender, it must give him or her fair opportunity to adduce any relevant financial information and to make appropriate submissions.

When considering these principles, it becomes clear that the imposition of costs is not to be viewed as punitive, hence its discussion here in Chapter 5, as opposed to Chapter 2. There is no doubt that many offenders feel that the award of costs against them is punitive – the fact that different payments, such as a fine, compensation, and costs all end up in different 'pots' once they have been paid, makes no difference to the person who is ordered to make the payment.

As any application for costs has to be considered in the context of the offender's means, their punitive bite, inevitable albeit theoretically unintended, should be limited – indeed, it is open to the court not to award costs if they do not feel it is appropriate to do so. Often this occurs where an offender is sentenced to immediate custody,[57] or has been remanded in custody prior to a non-custodial sentence, and therefore not in a position to be earning money to pay off the costs,[58] or the individual has straitened financial circumstances. Similarly, withholding costs can be a mechanism used by the court to express disapproval of prosecutorial decisions or processes (e.g. delay, or not accepting a plea to a lesser offence that the court views as reasonable).

Where an offender's personal circumstances mean that it would be unfair to require them to pay the whole sum of the costs sought, Judges will calculate a 'manageable' figure, and payment will be allowed over a period of time, as the Judge ordered for JSP:[59]

> You are to pay a contribution to Prosecution costs of £2000. You can either pay the whole lot off in 6 months/4 months etc or you can ask to

56 This principle was affirmed in *BPS Advertising Limited v London Borough of Barnet* [2006] EWHC 3335 (Admin).
57 *Wogui* [2013] EWCA Crim 1483, at [9]–[11].
58 *Rakib* [2011] EWCA Crim 870, at [45].
59 *R v JSP*, Isleworth Crown Court, 5th January 2018.

pay in monthly instalments. But that is only a fifth [of the costs incurred by the Prosecution] and that may be somewhat generous of me, but I think that £2000 is the just figure.

As well as reparation made to an individual victim through compensation – compulsorily made to victims generally through the victim surcharge, and discretionarily made to the state through costs – there are also mechanisms for making reparation to the wider community affected by an offence. This is seen particularly in the context of Community Orders and Suspended Sentence Orders, where unpaid work is a commonly attached requirement.

Community and Suspended Sentence Orders

An example of unpaid work being deployed in this way was seen when a Judge was sentencing JF for breaching an SSO, as referred to in Chapter 3.[60] That SSO had been imposed as a result of her behaviour after the break-down of her marriage and consequent alcoholism. She was unable to come to terms with the end of her marriage, and the fact that the children lived with their father in the former matrimonial home. She went round to the house, threatened to kill the children, assaulted one of the children, and assaulted the arresting officer. Due to her only having one previous conviction at that time, the sentencing Judge had imposed an SSO. She had then breached this by assaulting two further police officers when they attended a call from staff to remove her from a train on which she was extremely intoxicated and shouting abuse. In sentencing her to a Community Order for the new offences, which consisted of an unpaid work requirement, and adding further Rehabilitation Activity Requirement days to her original SSO for the breach, the Judge noted:

> In terms of the assaults on the police do not underestimate what you did to those officers. You should be thoroughly ashamed. It is time for you to behave more responsibly. I accept you entered a guilty plea at the first opportunity and I accept that the maximum sentence would be 6 months' imprisonment, and reduce it accordingly.
> [...]
> You will do 120 hours' unpaid work. I appreciate that you are a working woman and you have other things to do but you need to repay society. You will pay costs of £340, a statutory surcharge in the appropriate amount and compensation to each officer in sum of £50.

60 *R v JF*, Chelmsford Crown Court, 31st August 2016; see page 74 also.

This sentencing exercise demonstrates reparation through two methods – direct financial compensation to the police officers, one of whom suffered scratches and the other of whom was kicked in the chest, combined with reparation to the wider community by way of an unpaid work requirement.

Even beyond the specifying of physical labour in the local area (an unpaid work requirement often involves community projects such as communal gardening spaces) many would observe that Community Orders and Suspended Sentence Orders are construed as reparative to the community as a whole. This reparation is achieved indirectly by virtue of those on whom such orders are imposed having lower recidivism rates after completion of the order than other types of sentence. As the Orders result in a lower re-offending rate than sentences of imprisonment, and ultimately the best reparation to the community would be to have a law-abiding member, it can be argued that by their very nature they have the capacity to be more intrinsically reparative than imprisonment.

Some ancillary orders like compensation are directly reparative – restoring to the victim the financial value (or a part of it) of the item or money taken from them. Sometimes compensation involves putting a financial value on something with no monetary value, such as injuries, distress etc. That can be fundamentally problematic, and some would argue does not in fact provide reparation for the harm caused, simply an arbitrary monetary equation of the harm done.

What some would argue the system is currently missing, however, is the possibility to use restorative justice as a wholly diversionary reparative measure in cases where it is appropriate. At the moment, in the adult justice system, the possibility of restorative justice is only available as part of the sentencing stage disposal – i.e. it only becomes an option once the offender has already pleaded guilty,[61] when the Judge can then adjourn the sentencing for restorative justice to take place.[62]

Restorative justice

Restorative justice ('RJ') is a term with many different methods under its umbrella – something that can be seen as both its strength and its downfall.[63]

---

61 Restorative justice would only usually be used where an offender has pleaded guilty, as if they do not accept their guilt and so have pleaded not guilty and been convicted by a jury, they may be unlikely to be willing to enter into the spirit of restorative justice.

62 Para 5, Schedule 16 to the Crime and Courts Act 2013 inserted s.1ZA into the Powers of the Criminal Courts (Sentencing) Act 2000 – see more below.

63 Daly, K. (2016) What is Restorative Justice? Fresh Answers to a Vexed Question, *Victims and Offenders*, 11, pp. 9–29, at p. 22, suggests that the concept has become 'too capacious and imprecise'.

Daly describes it as a 'justice mechanism'.[64] Broadly, it can be described as a mechanism that seeks to provide an opportunity for the offender to provide reparation, but without quantification of the financial value or damage of items or experiences. However, the very concept itself has suffered from identity problems, with Daly remarking that 'the definitional problem is aggregating all the individual understandings into a coherent whole'.[65]

The theoretical underpinning, however, is identified by Johnstone, who notes that where crime is a violation of a person (as opposed to perpetrated against the state), a useful solution is 'repairing the harm and healing the trauma caused by crime'.[66]

Daly, however, concludes her 2016 article with a definition of her own:[67]

> Restorative justice is a contemporary justice mechanism to address crime, disputes, and bounded community conflict. The mechanism is a meeting (or several meetings) of affected individuals, facilitated by one or more impartial people. Meetings can take place at all phases of the criminal process – pre-arrest, diversion from court, pre-sentence, and post-sentence – as well as for offending or conflicts not reported to the police. Specific practices will vary, depending on context, but are guided by rules and procedures that align with what is appropriate in the context of the crime, dispute, or bounded conflict.

I would suggest this definition covers all of the aspects which lead its proponents to argue that it should take a greater role in the criminal justice system in England, and that if it were permitted to do so, there would be the possibility for real change for offenders who are currently trapped within a 'revolving door' system.

The Restorative Justice Council, a third-sector organisation in England which provides the membership body for restorative practices, provides six principles of restorative practice:[68] restoration, voluntarism, impartiality, safety, accessibility, and empowerment.

As this book has sought to show, the criminal justice system is a fundamentally human affair – and it is humanity around which restorative justice

---

64 *Ibid*, at p. 9.
65 *Ibid*, at p. 11.
66 Johnstone, G. (2008) 'The agendas of the restorative justice movement' in H. Miller (Ed.), Restorative justice: From theory to practice (pp. 59–79). Bingley, England: Emerald Group, at p. 67.
67 Daly (2016), at p. 21.
68 https://restorativejustice.org.uk/sites/default/files/The%20RJC%27s%20Principles%20of %20Restorative%20Practice.pdf [accessed 24th November 2020].

mechanisms are focussed. They are interested in interaction and dialogue – aspects which the current English sentencing process suppresses and denies, partly out of practical necessity in an over-stretched and under-funded system. Nonetheless, RJ is not a panacea, as is returned to below.

At what stage is there a role for restorative justice?

RJ is available for adult offenders as part of a conditional caution,[69] however, its use at that stage falls outside of the scope of this book, as cautions and conditional cautions are out-of-court disposals and are used instead of a person being charged with an offence in the first place.

There is an option for RJ as part of the sentencing process where an offender has been convicted through the criminal justice process.[70] Despite the Government stating in the Green Paper 'Breaking the Cycle: Effective Punishment, Rehabilitation and Sentencing of Offenders' in 2010 that the use of RJ should be increased for appropriate offences, aimed especially at improving victim satisfaction,[71] it is not known how often sentences are being deferred specifically for RJ activities.[72]

This option is found in s.7 of the Sentencing Act 2020.[73] That section makes it explicit that the courts can use their existing power to defer sentence post-conviction to allow for a restorative justice activity to take place by imposing an RJ requirement. Alternatively the court might adjourn sentence to allow for an RJ activity to take place,[74] providing that all who would be participants in the RJ give their consent.[75] Within the statute, RJ is defined as an activity:[76]

---

69 S.22(3)(b) CJA 03.
70 Fn 1.
71 Ministry of Justice (2010) Breaking the Cycle: Effective Punishment, Rehabilitation and Sentencing of Offenders, Cm 7972, at p. 22.
72 A Freedom of Information request was made to the Ministry of Justice asking how many sentences had been deferred for a restorative justice requirement to take place under the relevant section in 2019 – the response was that it would be too costly to provide the information.
73 Formerly s.1ZA PCC(S)A 00.
74 As noted earlier in this book, the key difference between adjourning sentence and deferring sentence is that a deferral can only be for up to six months, and it is usual for the defendant to be given conditions by which they must abide, in order to receive a shorter sentence at the deferred hearing. An adjournment can be for as long a period as the court decides, and the only conditions on the defendant will be any conditions attached to their bail. They cannot be required, as in a deferred sentence, to participate in particular activities or refrain from other activities which are separate from, and unrelated to, their bail conditions.
75 S.7(2) SA 20.
76 S.7(1) SA 20.

(a) where the participants consist of, or include, the offender and one or more of the victims,[77]
(b) which aims to maximise the offender's awareness of the impact of the offending concerned on the victims, and
(c) which gives an opportunity to a victim or victims to talk about, or by other means express experience of, the offending and its impact.

Should greater use be encouraged?

There remain questions about the most effective models for the deployment of restorative justice; in England an in-person meeting with a facilitator is the usual method, though 'indirect' mediation (sometimes called 'shuttle mediation') has also been used.[78] A seven-year study commissioned by the Ministry of Justice ran from 2001 to 2008, which reported in four parts, and used an experimental model to randomly assign victims and offenders willing to participate in restorative justice to a control group (no restorative justice undertaken) or an experimental group (restorative justice undertaken) in one programme that offered conferencing (JRC). In two other programmes, one that offered direct mediation, indirect mediation, and conferencing (CONNECT), and one that offered direct and indirect mediation (REMEDI),[79] there were matched control and comparison groups sampled.[80]

The fourth part of the study, albeit with a small sample size, showed that those offenders who participated in restorative justice committed statistically significantly fewer offences (in terms of reconvictions) in the subsequent two years than offenders in the control group. There was no statistically significant change in the likelihood of reconviction over the next two years, or in the severity of reconviction. All the JRC groups (summed together) showed a lower cost of convictions versus a control group. Results for REMEDI and CONNECT were not statistically significant.[81] Costs of convictions included the costs to potential future victims and criminal justice costs.

There were significant relationships between several measures of re-offending and offender views about the conference. In particular a

77 S.7(5) SA 20 enlarges that 'victim' means a victim of, or other person affected by, the offending concerned.
78 Shapland, J. et al. (2008) Does restorative justice affect reconviction? The fourth report from the evaluation of three schemes, Ministry of Justice Research Series 10/08, London: Ministry of Justice, at p. i.
79 Although the use of RJ in the youth justice system is not covered in this book, it should be noted that some of the cases included within this study did involve young offenders.
80 *Ibid*, at p. i and ii.
81 *Ibid*, at p. iii.

number of factors were all significantly and positively related to decreased reconviction,[82] namely, the extent to which the offenders felt the conference had made them realise the harm done; whether the offender wanted to meet the victim; the extent to which the offender was observed to be actively involved in the conference; and how useful offenders felt the conference had been. This highlights why care must be taken when selecting those cases and offenders who are suitable for restorative justice. Various accounts of the researchers showed that not all offenders took responsibility for their actions, even in an RJ conference to which they had explicitly consented, though a large proportion did apologise to victims for their actions.[83]

The overall response to engagement in RJ by both offenders and victims was one of satisfaction: [84]

> Not everyone was entirely satisfied, however, with 26 per cent of JRC offenders and 34 per cent of victims showing some element of dissatisfaction about one aspect – but there were only six offenders and six victims who were dissatisfied overall (out of 152 offenders and 216 victims interviewed). As many as 74 per cent of JRC offenders and 78 per cent of victims would definitely or probably recommend restorative justice to others for similar offences (11% of offenders and 9% of victims were not sure whether they would or not; 3% of offenders and 5% of victims would probably not). Very few had been put off by their experience (10% of JRC offenders and 10% of victims would probably or definitely not recommend it). Dissatisfaction revolved around disputes between victim and offender regarding the offence, or difficulties in communication.

Perhaps unsurprisingly in a voluntary activity, the apparently high efficacy of restorative justice can be linked to the self-selection bias inherent in those who are willing to participate in a restorative justice technique, and further, those who are willing to then engage with research on the topic.[85] This, however, does not mean that it should be side-lined – the empirical research in England detailed above shows that RJ can have strong positive

---

82 *Ibid*, at p. iv.
83 Shapland et al. (2006) Restorative Justice in Practice: The second report from the evaluation of three schemes, University of Sheffield: Centre for Criminological Research, at pp. 55–58.
84 Shapland et al. (2007) Restorative justice: the views of victims and offenders: The third report from the evaluation of three schemes, London: Ministry of Justice, at pp. 46–47.
85 Latimer, J., Dowden, C., and Muise, D. (2005) The Effectiveness of Restorative Justice Practices: A Meta-Analysis, *The Prison Journal*, 85(2), pp. 127–144.

effects when used for the right victims and offenders,[86] in a careful and structured way.

Conclusion

Reparation is seen in almost every sentencing exercise – though most often as the imposition of costs and a victim surcharge. Focussing on reparation to the criminal justice system through financial means, however, can be impractical in a system that deals disproportionately with those who have very little financially, and the requirement to pay costs and a surcharge has not been shown to have any link to a reduction in recidivism.[87] Instead of working together with the aim to reduce offending, reparation has become simply a matter of administrative convenience; a way to claw back a tiny proportion of the gargantuan costs of the criminal justice system. Restorative justice, whilst certainly not a panacea, nor appropriate for every offence and offender/victim combination, offers a more meaningful way to reparation for some groups of offenders and victims, with the additional possibility of a reduction in future offending.

---

86 Though even the sort of offences for which RJ should be offered is contested; whilst many would argue that in offences of fatal violence, RJ between the deceased's family and the offender would not be appropriate, Walters relates a case study in which it was found to be effective: Walters, M. A. (2015) 'I thought "he's a monster" … [but] he was just… normal': Examining the therapeutic benefits of restorative justice for homicide, *British Journal of Criminology*, 55(6), pp. 1207–1225.

87 The author is not aware of any research that has been done exploring whether there is any link between these monetary aspects of sentence and recidivism.

Concluding thoughts

This book has sought to illustrate the variety of judicial approaches to sentencing. Even within the increasingly constraining legislative framework, Judges and magistrates are seen going to real efforts to construct sentences that give meaning to some or all of the purposes of sentencing found in s.57(2) SA 20, as well as considering the positions of defendants, victims, and members of the wider community.

By using sentencing remarks from cases that have been heard in Magistrates' Courts and Crown Courts in England, it is has been possible to examine the theory through the prism of practice. Sentencing remarks in real cases also bring into stark relief some of the difficult sentencing decisions that Judges make – even where discretion has been severely limited in pursuit of consistency, there are still human beings central to that process, and the variety of considerations and articulations seen in this book reflect that that is borne in mind by many Judges.

Even where a sentence has a theoretically attractive underpinning, IPP has demonstrated that the gulf between practice and theory can be vast. It is only when examining the 'real life' effects of IPP that it is possible to see why the theory could not be seamlessly implemented for those men and women who received it. Conversely, in fact, it has caused, and continues to cause, many to be detained long after it is likely that they are no longer a danger, whilst not offering meaningful rehabilitation opportunities to those who remain 'dangerous'.

Brief considerations of ways in which some of the theoretical purposes in s.57(2) are put into practice in other jurisdictions allow us to consider that there are different ways of prioritising objectives in sentencing practice. Whether or not that priority is explicitly articulated within the legislation, or whether it is demonstrated through, for example, the retention of the death penalty in America, or the reluctance to use long terms of imprisonment in Nordic countries, different approaches enlighten the exploration of the English system.

DOI: 10.4324/9781003201625-102

Index

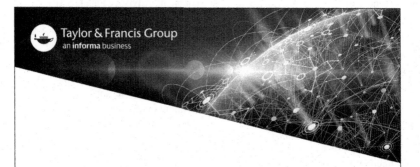